Praise for
A Calling to Care

"In an era of navigating the increasing demands and needs of students in higher education, our actions and reactions can become fragmented and situational. This collection of writings brilliantly reminds readers of the complexities as well as the necessity of providing holistic care, both institutionally and individually, for our students. The authors invite us to consider care beyond sweet sentiments and to engage students in meaningful interactions essential for flourishing in all aspects of their lives."

—Kris Hansen-Kieffer, Vice Provost and Dean of Students, Messiah College, and former President of ACSD

"This text is a clarion call to focus our limited resources on an ancient yet timely component of formation—taking care of those we educate and teaching them to take care of themselves. Herrmann, Riedel, and the editorial team have provided us direct access to relevant voices from across academia that inspire, challenge, and instruct us on how to transfer our good intentions into impactful actions. This resource is bound to become essential reading for all of us in higher education and could not have come at a better time."

—Stephen Beers, Associate Professor of Higher Education and Vice President for Student Development, Athletics, and Facilities, John Brown University, former President of ACSD

"In the late 1800s, the student development profession emerged out of the faculty as a way to care for students beyond the classroom. *A Calling to Care* is a reminder of our roots and an articulation of that vision for the twenty-first century. The wide-ranging voices of seasoned and young professionals who are both practitioners and scholars make this monograph a worthy investment of study for those who truly care for the students on university campuses."

—Jay Barnes, President, Bethel University

"In this battlefield of academe filled with casualties, we desperately need this book in order to learn how to care and heal in deeper and more complicated ways. Gracefully, the authors provide us with myriad sources of wisdom and a variety of perspectives about how we can join with Jesus in carefully mending our students, our institutions, and our own hearts and souls."

—Perry L. Glanzer, Professor of Educational Foundations and Resident Scholar, Baylor Institute for Studies of Religion, Baylor University

A CALLING TO
CARE

VOLUME 2 IN THE ACSD MONOGRAPH SERIES

ACSD Association for Christians
in Student Development

A CALLING TO
CARE

NURTURING COLLEGE STUDENTS
TOWARD WHOLENESS

EDITORS | TIMOTHY W. HERRMANN & KIRSTEN D. RIEDEL

COEDITORS | EMILIE K. HOFFMAN, JESSICA L. MARTIN,
KELLY A. YORDY & HANNAH M. PICK

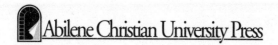

Abilene Christian University Press

A CALLING TO CARE

Nurturing College Students toward Wholeness

ACU PRESS

Copyright © 2018 by Timothy W. Herrmann, Kirsten D. Riedel, Emilie K. Hoffman Jessica L. Martin, Kelly A. Yordy, and Hannah M. Pick

ISBN 978-1-68426-160-4

Printed in the United States of America

Cataloging in Publication data is on file at the Library of Congress, Washington, DC.

Cover design by ThinkPen Design
Interior text design by Sandy Armstrong, Strong Design

For information contact:
Abilene Christian University Press
ACU Box 29138
Abilene, Texas 79699

1-877-816-4455
www.acupressbooks.com

18 19 20 21 22 23 / 7 6 5 4 3 2 1

The publication of this book has been sponsored by the Association for Christians in Student Development.

The mission of the Association for Christians in Student Development is to equip and challenge members to infuse their Christian faith into student development practice and scholarship.

CONTENTS

Acknowledgments 11

Introduction 13
    Timothy W. Herrmann

Chapter One 21
    What Will Save the World?:
    Caring for the World We Cannot Save
    Miroslav Volf

Chapter Two 37
    Mentorship as Care for Emerging Adulthood:
    A Conversation with Sharon Daloz Parks and Timothy W. Herrmann
    Sharon Daloz Parks and Timothy W. Herrmann

Chapter Three 55
    Nel Noddings's Ethic of Care:
    Thoughts for Student Development Educators
    Kelly A. Yordy

Chapter Four 77
    Teaching Students to Care for Themselves
    Kirsten D. Riedel, Emilie K. Hoffman, Jessica L. Martin

Chapter Five 103
    A Call for Holistic Intellectual Care of University Students:
    An Essay for the Twenty-First-Century Academy
    Anita Fitzgerald Henck

Chapter Six 119
    Solidarity and Mutuality as an Ethic of Care *with* Students of Color
    Tabatha L. Jones Jolivet and Karen A. Longman

Chapter Seven 141
    Call(s) and Care(s) in Collegiate Ministry
    Donald D. Opitz

Chapter Eight... 163

    Caring Enough to Mentor College Students with Disabilities

    Roger D. Wessel and Larry Markle

Chapter Nine... 179

    Christ-Centered Approaches to Address Sexual Violence
    and Pornography

    John D. Foubert

Chapter Ten... 193

    Higher Education as an Exemplar of Care:
    Creating a Campus Culture of Care

    Timothy W. Herrmann

Editors... 215

Contributors... 219

ACKNOWLEDGMENTS

Producing a volume such as this one necessarily involves the assistance of a number of people, and the monograph you hold in your hands is no exception. First, we want to thank the Association for Christians in Student Development, especially the executive committee, for their vision in commissioning a series of four monographs, of which this volume is the second. Past presidents Steve Beers and Kris Hansen-Kieffer, current president Edee Schulze, and scholarship chair Drew Moser have been instrumental in bringing this project to fruition. Without their help and support, this project could not have happened. Their collaboration was a significant encouragement to the editorial team. Perhaps more importantly, their actions provided continued evidence that the association is committed to promoting scholarship, contributing to the conversation regarding college student development, and providing thought leadership within the academy. This investment is both inspiring and laudable, and we are indeed grateful.

Next, we would like to thank Todd Ream, who coordinated the 2017–18 Taylor University Higher Education Symposium with the theme *A Calling to Care: Nurturing College Students toward Wholeness.* Three chapters of this volume emerged directly from that event. Without Todd's energy, hard work, and innovative thinking, neither the symposium nor this volume would have been possible. We also would be remiss not to thank Skip Trudeau, Taylor University vice president for student development, who also provided tremendous assistance in this project.

Most importantly, we want to thank the authors of the various chapters. We believe that each chapter provides an important contribution to the discussion of how we may best address the complex needs of college students. Special thanks go to the symposium plenary speakers Miroslav Volf, Sharon Daloz Parks, and John Foubert, whose three chapters form the backbone of this volume. All have provided truly exceptional chapters and were extremely helpful in the formulation of this document.

And finally, to the student development educators—the practitioners who work so diligently, skillfully, and selflessly for the emerging adults at the center of this volume—thank you for the efforts, investments, and care you contribute to these young lives. It is our sincerest hope that the material contained in this monograph will serve you well as you seek to serve students.

INTRODUCTION

TIMOTHY W. HERRMANN

Taylor University

Writing and compiling this monograph about care has been an interesting project, to say the least. When addressing a topic like this, writers are forced to examine their own thoughts about the subject as well as their own experiences—both as caregivers and as receivers of care. Because we have all both received and given care, we have had to work not to allow our own experiences to be the sole definer of care. Additionally, because care is such a broad concept with roots in so many disciplines and traditions, it is harder than one might imagine to settle on a singular working definition. Capturing or defining the concept and practice of care has been remarkably like Rens Bod's and Julia Kursell's efforts to define the humanities. Invoking Augustine's thoughts on time, Bod and Kursell (2015) resorted to suggesting that "if you don't ask, we know, but if you ask, we are left empty handed" (p. 337). Though admittedly a challenging task, the good news is that I do not think we have been left empty handed.

If we assume that the Good Shepherd represents a model of what it means to care, we quickly come to the understanding that care is actually a bit of a paradox—like the oft-used relational descriptor, "Well, it's complicated." Is it care when Jesus heals the blind, or is it care when he tells the rich young ruler to sell all he has and give the money to the poor? Does care look like Jesus presiding over the Last Supper, or is it telling Peter to "get thee behind me, Satan"? The truth is that all of these examples represent care. Sometimes care looks like gentleness, and sometimes care looks like accountability and correction. As an editorial team, we decided early in the process of developing this monograph that care was too rich, too varied, and too nuanced a concept to allow us to provide a simple, straightforward definition that would fit the assortment of topics addressed here. Therefore, as you will see in the following pages, we have allowed the various contributors to define the concept or highlight its most important qualities in the manner that best aligns with the context of their topic. We believe this tactic was the appropriate one, and we trust that the various approaches and treatments contained in this volume will enrich and sharpen your own understanding of such an incredibly important idea.

It has become almost a mantra among those who work in colleges and universities—"These are difficult days in higher education." We are burdened by issues of finance, state and federal support, institutional and individual identity, free speech, racial and social equity, technology, curriculum, and even purpose. These are indeed difficult days in higher education, and these troubles do not just threaten the well-being of higher education, but they sometimes sap the energy, resources, and even resolve to do what is best for those whose welfare has been entrusted to us.

Despite current realities and the differing perspectives held by those who work in higher education, there is one outcome of higher education upon which all educators and educational leaders surely agree: students ought to leave college stronger—intellectually, emotionally, relationally, and spiritually—than they came. While there are many different ways to envision the correct means to this end, it is clear that its accomplishment requires more than appropriate curricula, programs, facilities, and resources; to properly educate college students requires a concern for and commitment to a holistic vision of their care.

In keeping with the vision called for above, this volume explores the centrality of caring for students and making our campuses places that build and nurture them toward health, wholeness, and purpose. This monograph proposes that creating environments and conditions of care is an elemental component of the academy that must be attended to in substantive and meaningful ways. This suggestion is not for a new code or professional standard of student care, helpful as such things can be. Rather, it is intended as an encouragement to college and university leaders to enthusiastically and competently embrace these purposes for the good of their students, their institutions, their communities, and the world. As referenced later in this volume, Milo Rediger, former president of Taylor University, used to assert that "love prompts more than the law demands." His reminder may be even more important in these contentious days than when it was first uttered decades ago. While professional competence is a must, competent care offered without genuine love and regard for students will accomplish little. We hope then that we are prompting those people who are already committed professionals to redouble their commitment to the ancient and timeless purposes of the university and their determination to translate these ancient standards into forms relevant to the modern higher educational milieu.

Sharon Daloz Parks, contributor to this volume and long revered by those who work with college students, suggests in her modern classic *Big Questions, Worthy Dreams* (2011) that colleges and universities must be, at once, places of journey or pilgrimage and places of hospitality—homes for our students. This language seems familiar to us because it hearkens back to Nevitt Sanford's notion of challenge and support and other foundational models of college student development. In addition to being familiar, it also provides a simple organizing structure for institutions and individuals who are called to care for college students. With this idea—or, perhaps more properly, educational ideal—in mind, this monograph considers what it means at both the institutional and individual levels to care well for college students.

Our exploration of the "calling to care" has led us down some lovely and profitable paths. The fourteen contributors to this volume understand this calling uniquely and therefore have approached their contributions to this conversation in distinctive ways. As you read the various contributions, you will do well to remember that each represents a different voice in this conversation. Further, these authors have traveled unique experiential, educational, spiritual, and vocational pathways that mark them and shape the way they understand care as well as the way they understand the various topics and issues that they cover here. Thus, our intent is that this volume should be considered a thoughtful and informed discussion rather than a unified, integrated statement on the care of college students. As an editor of this work and as one who is imperfectly committed (but committed nonetheless) to lifelong learning, it has been a privilege and a gift to have the opportunity to sort through and study each contribution. Clearly this experience has been an enriching and nourishing one, and we trust that as you read these pages, you will experience the same sense of blessing.

In Chapter One, a foundational segment of this monograph, noted author and scholar Miroslav Volf provides a theological exploration of our theme as he considers just what it means to "care for the world we cannot save." His fascinating and challenging comments will help you to consider the very idea of care in a "stained" world. Though he addresses the topic at a deep level, you will find his thoughts and ideas to be immensely meaningful and even practical in formulating a basis for an ethic of care.

The second chapter is unique in this volume because rather than being a traditionally composed essay, it represents an edited manuscript of a public conversation between Dr. Sharon Daloz Parks and myself. This discussion of mentorship as a critical form of care for emerging adults rehearses and expands many of Parks's ideas that have been deeply helpful to so many of us in our service to students. In this regard, it is no mistake or matter of convenience that accounts for the inclusion of Parks in this monograph. For decades her career and writing have compellingly demonstrated the power and the promise of mentoring and mentoring communities. Her ideas, which were broadly and enthusiastically received in the early years of my career four decades ago, have lost none of their appeal to younger educators. It was remarkable to witness Taylor University graduate students' responses to her visit to our campus in 2017. They were deeply drawn to her and the ideas that she presented. While admittedly it was a joy to interact with Dr. Parks, it was even more exciting to see the effect she had on our students—she is a remarkable person whose life and manner represent an incredible illustration of what she writes and teaches and, ultimately, what it means to be an educator who cares.

It is impossible to explore the concept of care for college students without considering Nel Noddings's ethics of care. In Chapter Three, Kelly Yordy thoughtfully unpacks Noddings's most important ideas regarding relational care and their connection to the theme of this book. These ideas provide critical philosophical and practical understandings that help us to dig deeper into the meaning and limits of care.

A core goal of any form of education is teaching our students to "do for themselves" and enhancing their ability and desire to act independently. This aim is no less essential in the realm of care than it is in any other. Thus, helping our students to understand and practice proper self-care is crucial. From a theological standpoint, it has been said that proper regard for oneself is prerequisite to one's ability to properly love and care for one's neighbors (McKnight, 2013). However, anyone who has worked with students—trying to move them from dependent to independent states—knows that this endeavor can be challenging. In Chapter Four, "Teaching Students to Care for Themselves," Kirsten Riedel, Emilie Hoffman, and Jessica Martin use the literature and their own work with students to provide an immensely helpful primer on student self-care. This discussion will guide and inform our efforts to nurture students toward holistic health and independence by cultivating their ability to care for themselves.

If the heart and most essential purpose of the university is to promote student learning, then we must think properly about what it means to offer effective and well-conceived intellectual care. Anita Henck, an experienced student affairs practitioner, faculty member, and now dean of the school of education at Azusa Pacific University, offers an insightful reflection on intellectual care and the necessity of maintaining its centrality in the educational endeavor. The ideas and understandings she offers in Chapter Five are critical for those who educate college students—in the traditional classroom or outside.

In Chapter Six, Tabatha Jones Jolivet and Karen Longman discuss solidarity and mutuality as an ethic of care with students of color. It seems to go without saying that this topic is an absolutely essential element of any contemporary conversation regarding the care of college students. The insights offered in this chapter will not only help us to provide more meaningful support for our students of color but will also help us to become more thoughtful, informed, and committed as we try to foster more equitable, more hospitable, and more empowering campus communities.

It could be said that this entire monograph is focused on ministering to others, as "to minister" is actually a synonym for care. In Chapter Seven, Don Opitz considers the elements of care offered from a foundation of faith. In particular, he reminds us of the dangerous tendency of making careless body-soul and sacred-secular distinctions. To this point, he helps us to more fully grasp the idea that everything we do as we care for others is, in reality, soul care.

Chapter Eight is another exploration of mentoring but, in this case, as a form of caring for students with disabilities. Roger Wessel and Larry Markle provide the legal and philosophical contexts for thoughtful mentoring of college students with disabilities and an explanation of how to create an ethic of care for students with disabilities on college campuses.

In the ninth chapter, John Foubert considers Christ-centered approaches to address sexual violence and pornography. Needless to say, these realities represent a troubling element of our culture and have also been at the forefront of current issues of concern in higher education. Foubert suggests that mentoring communities represent one of our best hopes for counteracting these developments.

The final chapter concludes with my own reflections on caring well for students. Additionally, the chapter discusses the current crisis of purpose facing higher education and considers how this may in fact present an opportunity for higher education to provide a model of care for the rest of the culture.

As suggested previously, this monograph was intended as an effort to create a conversation about how we can best nurture wholeness in the lives of college students. We are pleased to commend this book to you, and we trust that the work of these caring contributors will enrich your thinking about care and your work with college students.

References

Bod, R., & Kursell, J. (2015). Introduction: The humanities and the sciences. *Isis,*
    106, 337–340. doi:10.1086/681993

McKnight, S. (2013). *Sermon on the mount.* Grand Rapids, MI: Zondervan.

1

WHAT WILL SAVE THE WORLD?

Caring for the World We Cannot Save[1]

MIROSLAV VOLF

Yale Divinity School

I

It is *easy to change* the world; throw a rock at a masterpiece, as Ugo Ungaza Villegas did at Leonardo's *Mona Lisa* in 1956, or point a gun at a crowd and pull the trigger, and you will have changed the world, for the worse.

It is *hard to improve* the world, sometimes as hard as creating the painting that is so easy to vandalize or raising up children into people who are so easy to wound and kill.

---

[1] The key ideas in this essay were put together for the Nexus Institute Conference in November of 2016. I am grateful to Nexus Institute founder and president Rob Riemen for stimulating renewed exploration of this impossibly large but crucial theme. For the essays from the conference, see *Nexus* 74 (Breda: Nexus Institute, 2017), 71–82. Work on this essay was made possible by the support of the McDonald Agape Foundation and John Templeton Foundation, and its writing occasioned energetic conversation among the staff of the Yale Center for Faith & Culture, from which I benefited a great deal; Karin Fransen in particular helped with both the substance and the form of the essay. To all of them, an energetic intellectual community, I owe a debt of gratitude. I presented a version of the essay as a lecture on September 14, 2017, at Taylor University and revised it in light of the discussion there.

It is *impossible to save* the world—at least it is impossible for humans to do so if we give the word "save" anything close to the utopian sense we generally associate with the idea of saving the world.

The world needs improving because there is too much suffering and derogation, too much futile work and unsatisfying pleasure, too little self-forgetful care and genuine joy.

The world needs saving, for otherwise the entire blood-stained and tear-drenched history will remain unredeemed.

II

The conviction that we can save the world gained wide currency in the course of modernity. Most influential strands of this most consequential period in Western history affirmed the unambiguous basic goodness and perfectibility of human beings, stripped Jewish messianic and Christian eschatological hopes of their transcendent dimension and projected them onto the world process. What made plausible this Pollyannaish take on human beings and history was the signature achievement of modernity: the discovery of the method that assured progress in scientific knowledge and, consequently, an unprecedented pace of technological innovation. The marriage of technological prowess and anthropological optimism gave birth to a secular eschatological faith: a "vision of the human race, at last released from the empire of fate and from the enemies of its progress, advancing with a firm and sure step along the path of truth, virtue and happiness" (Lukes, 1995, p. 29–30). The improbable hope-dogma of this ersatz religion was this: "The right design and the final argument can be, must be, and will be found" (Bauman, 1993, p. 9).[2]

Modernity's faith in infinite progress and the final solution—following Hegel, some call it the "end of history" (Fukuyama, 1992)—never lacked sophisticated critics. The most perceptive of them did not zero in on the

---

[2] As an alternative to the "right design" and "final argument," it will not work to think of progress as open-ended, with no specified future in view. For then "progress" amounts to no more than "change," as we are unable to show that "progress is actually 'progressive,' unless we have some standard by which to judge" (Smith, 2016, p. 351).

obvious: modernity's colossal failures that shadowed its indubitable successes, like the imperialist project or the deadly global plague of multiple communist experiments. Instead, these critics uncovered the rot in modernity's strengths and exposed the ambivalence of its successes: exploitation and scandalous inequalities, shallowness of popular culture, unpredictable risks, ecological devastation, and more.[3] The general populace had its own ambivalences that only partly shadowed those of modernity's critics and defenders. It both celebrated and feared the times in which it lived, its moods swinging from optimism to pessimism and back, depending upon whether modernity's blessings or curses seemed to prevail.

As I write this essay, dystopian cultural moods predominate. Many find it easier to imagine the world crumbling "into the dust of this planet" than blossoming into a paradise or ending as a technological utopia. Contemporary gloom feeds on worrisome global realities: great and growing disparities in power, wealth, and skill; climate changes and devastation of the environment; weakening of local cultures under pressures of migration and global super-culture; the specter of human redundancy (emerging artificial intelligence!); the planetary reach of barbaric terror. All of these threats would be less worrisome were it not for a widespread sense that we live in a "runaway world."[4] Many are gripped by the feeling of frustrating impotence. Disaster is looming, and nobody is in charge.

Granted, cultural moods are not reliable indicators of the actual state of the world. Ours are not the darkest of all times, not by a long shot. For instance, levels of murderous violence have steadily gone down and average longevity has gone up, which is no small achievement.[5] Still, dystopian

---

[3] This is one of the main points of Stephen B. Smith's (2016) *Modernity and its discontents: Making and unmaking the bourgeois from Machiavelli to Bellow.* See Duflo, A., & Mosenkis, J. (2016, December 30). Why 2016 was actually one of the best years on record. *The Washington Post.*

[4] Giddens, A. (2010). *Runaway world: How globalization is reshaping our lives.* New York, NY: Routledge. The title notwithstanding, the book is rather optimistic about globalization.

[5] For a rather optimistic picture of the state of the world, see Pinker, S. (2011). *The better angels of our nature: Why violence has declined.* New York, NY: Penguin.

cultural winds are symptoms of a malady, reminders that the world has not come much nearer to salvation, especially so if it is true that we cannot be saved without thinking and feeling that we *are* saved. Stunning techno-logical advances and enormous increases in wealth notwithstanding, no utopia seems around the corner, not even around the faraway bend of a very long road. Why not?

———

In the second of his *Unfashionable Observations*, Friedrich Nietzsche observed that "living and being unjust are one and the same thing" (Nietzsche, trans. 1995, p. 107). The conclusion he drew from this dark observation is darker than the observation itself: "Every past is worthy of being condemned" (pp. 106–107) and of perishing. Consequently, it would have been better "if nothing came into being" (pp. 106–107). Who sits in judgment here? Not just "life," Nietzsche wrote, "that dark, driving, insatiable power that lusts after itself," whose judgment is "always merci-less, always unjust, because it has never flowed from the pure fountain of knowledge" (pp. 106–107). In most cases, he insisted, "the verdict would be the same, even if spoken by justice itself" (p. 107). The notion that every past deserves to perish did not originate with Nietzsche. He took it straight from Goethe's *Faust*, where it appears on the lips of Mephistopheles, a demon in Satan's service.[6] "To live is to be unjust" is a tenet of a resolutely anti-Christian creed. Surprisingly, perhaps, it is also a key conviction in the Christian take on the human condition.

Among theologians, the Protestant reformer Martin Luther is famous for celebrating the utter gratuity of God's love. Significantly, he affirmed the unconditionality of God's love while insisting on the pervasiveness and indelibility of human stain. Short of the radically new life in the world to come, humans cannot achieve a better moral and existential condition than to always remain both sinners and just at the same time, in every aspect of

---

[6] Arndt, W. (2001). *Faust.* New York, NY: W. W. Norton. Mephistopheles spoke these lines in the scene in the study, just after he had identified himself as "the spirit who always negates" (line 1338).

their being. No matter how much we improve, every one of our deeds bears a stain, and every one of them inserts itself into a stained world where it always benefits from and effects both blessings and curses.

A person need not embrace Luther's account of sin to affirm the indelibility and pervasiveness of human stain. A great twentieth-century Catholic theologian, Karl Rahner (1978), used a simple example to make the point. We cannot take a single bite into the soft flesh of a banana without being left with an aftertaste of the sin of the world, the sin of all the people that made that banana land half-peeled in our hand: the owners of the plantation and all those with whom the plantation owners jostle for space to make profit, the overworked and underpaid workers, the global traders and the transporters, the salespeople, even those who made the clothes we wore and the car we drove as we went grocery shopping. It would be easy to give a more extensive and fine-grained description of the net of sin into which consuming a banana pulls us, but the point is clear. Over everything we do and enjoy hover sighs of suffering and the self-satisfied laughter of selfish indifference and oppression.

As the example of the banana suggests, human stain always bears the stamp of a given time and place, but the stain itself is universal because it is an aspect of the human condition, tangled up with the character of our materiality, temporality, sociality, self-transcendence, and freedom. Stained as we are, we can mend but we cannot save—neither the world nor ourselves. Salvation will either come from outside the world or it will not come at all.

III

Nietzsche was as resolutely anti-modern as he was implacably anti-Christian, and partly for the same reasons. To see why, remember that, notwithstanding what I just wrote in the previous section, the Christian faith is not mainly about human stain and its indelibility but about the original and abiding goodness of God and, despite the stain, of the world God created. Modernity picked up, zeroed in on, and magnified a dimension of the Christian faith Nietzsche himself rejected in insisting on the injustice of living; indeed, he rejected the category of moral "goodness" itself.

According to the Genesis story of creation, before the disaster of the fall (Gen. 3), the world as God created it was good, even very good (Gen. 1). The "before" of creation's goodness is not only temporal; it is primarily ontological. More basic than the stain is that which the stain sullies. Far from canceling creation's goodness, the stain can appear as *stain* (rather than simply as an aspect of life itself) only on account of the creation's goodness. That is why from a Christian standpoint, despite the world's pervasive injustice, Mephistopheles and Nietzsche got it wrong: it would not have been better for the world not to have come into being.

Both the world's goodness and its salvation from the inerasable stain presuppose the goodness of the Creator. According to the Christian faith—and, in distinct ways, according to Judaism and Islam as well—all the long lines of human history in the end converge, not simply in some perfect state of the world, but in the world become "God's home among mortals," as John the Seer put it in the book of Revelation (21:3 NRSV). Behind this eschatological vision lies the conviction that the world's salvation must be and will be an act of "new creation." The claim is this: God created the world in the beginning out of nothing; God will create a new world in the end out of the old one. Both these creations that bookend and undergird the history of the cosmos are God's acts, fruits of God's goodness.

Modernity's faith in progress needs a critic like Nietzsche to keep it honest. Let me put it provocatively and controversially: If you believe that "nothing but the world can be the case," as Peter Sloterdijk (1993, p. 106) famously said was modernity's creed, you cannot believe that the world, this world or the world structured like ours, will be saved. Inversely, if you believe that the world can be and will be saved, you must believe that more than the world is the case.

—⁓—

Though we cannot save the world, we can *improve* it or "mend" it, to use a more modest term at home in Jewish religious tradition. And that is where care comes in. In a sense, the entire human history is also a history of mending and improving the world. Over the centuries since the beginning of modernity, technological innovation, market economy, and modern statecraft, for instance, have increased the health, wealth, and longevity of billions, thereby immensely improving the state of the world. Of course, improvements are shadowed by damages, to individuals and to the entire ecosystem. Technological innovation, moreover, creates incalculable risks, many of them unknown; we know that some storm is always on the horizon, but we do not always know whether it will unleash itself upon us and, if it does, what the damage will be.[7]

New technologies and modern social institutions are not the only sources of the world's improvements. Countless daily acts of love—simple expressions of care—are, arguably, more significant (just as the love between spouses is more important for marital happiness than all the amenities their house can possibly have). To improve the state of a single person, to give her a cup of cold water (as Jesus famously said in Matt. 10:42), is to improve the state of the world. And yet the individuals who mend the world are also individuals who damage the world. Even that cup of cold water can be a "poisoned" gift—a gift because it quenches the thirst and restores life, but poisoned because in helping we often humiliate, violate, or aim to exploit. Most givers are a bit—perhaps only a very tiny bit—like the imperialist Mr. Kurtz of Joseph Conrad's *Heart of Darkness*: in their very generosity they are also evildoers invested in seeing themselves and being seen as some weightily consequential "Immensity ruled by an august Benevolence" (Conrad, 1899/1990, p. 46).[8] The struggle for the purity of care is the struggle for improvement of the world.

We can and must improve the world. But all our improvements are ambivalent, marked by the indelible stain and effecting both blessings and curses. The great challenge for us is not to save the world; only God can

[7] On risk society, see Beck, U. (1992). *Risk society: Towards a new modernity*. London, UK: Sage.

[8] Conrad, J. (1990). *Heart of darkness*. New York, NY: Dover Publications. For a pessimistic—overly pessimistic, I would argue—reading of all gift-giving, see Bourdieu, P. (1997). Marginalia: Some additional notes on the gift. In A. D. Schrift (Ed.), *The logic of the gift: Toward an ethic of generosity* (pp. 231–241). New York, NY: Routledge.

do that. Our challenge is to protect and enhance the flourishing of all life in a world we cannot save.

———

Many critics of the conviction that God is the source and goal of all reality believe that attachment to God makes the practice of care for the world incoherent, that it subverts ordinary human flourishing. Love for infinite God drowns out love for finite creatures. Obedience to the first great commandment of monotheistic religions—the command to love God with everything we are and have—makes the fulfillment of the second great commandment—to love our neighbors as ourselves—impossible; it always ends up twisting the love for neighbor into indifference (if love for God suppresses the care for neighbor) or hatred (if we feel that the care for the neighbor is robbing us of the ability to love God adequately). We may try to love God *and* neighbor, but we always end up loving either God *or* neighbor.

This is a big charge tied up with many difficult questions, to which I can here give only a short and simple answer: love for God does not negate love for the world but purifies and enhances it.[9] Let me try to make plausible this sweeping claim by taking a closer look at just one small, albeit important, aspect of care for finite things: our enjoyment of them. It would be easy to make a parallel argument to the one below about the creation and distribution of goods, both important aspects of care for finite goods: rather than undermining creation and equitable distribution of goods, the love for God, Creator and lover of all creatures, underwrites it.

IV

For all life to flourish, we need to do much to improve the state of the world. But it is possible to benefit from myriads of the world's genuine improvements and still not flourish, not even feel happy, and that is not just because of the inescapable shadows of these improvements which I

---

[9] See pages 185–196 from Adams, R. M. (1999). *Finite and infinite goods: A framework for ethics*. Oxford, UK: Oxford University Press.

mentioned earlier. We accomplish this extraordinary feat of self-subversion daily: we receive without feeling enriched by the gift; we even give without being ennobled by this most human of our acts. As to our pleasures, they are fleeting, fickle, and often self-canceling: we often feel shortchanged if we do not flatten into mere fun what could have been genuine and deep joys, and we do so even when we know that fun, "a thin pleasure, laid on as a coating" (Seneca, 65/1979), lasts only as long as it lasts and leaves us empty, whereas joy irradiates our past and future with meaning. Truly to flourish we need both to improve the world and to learn to experience the world in a new way. Love for God underwrites and enhances both, largely by shaping the character and expanding the scope of our care.

—∿∿—

The mother of all temptations, equally hard to resist in abundance and in want, is to believe and act as if human beings lived by bread alone, as if our entire lives should revolve around the creation, improvement, distribution, and securitization of worldly goods. Succumb to that temptation, and the best you can do in terms of enjoyment is to have fun; deeper joy will escape you. The first is not always bad, but the second is much richer.

"Turn these stones into bread," the tempter taunted Jesus, famished after a forty-day fast in the wilderness. Jesus resisted, responding, "One does not live by bread alone, but by every word that comes from the mouth of God" (Matt. 4:4 NRSV). Jesus was quoting the Hebrew Bible. Moses, the great deliverer and lawgiver, first uttered these words to the children of Israel as a summary of the main lesson they were to have learned in the course of the forty years of wandering in the wilderness before entering the Promised Land. Bread was what they needed in the wilderness; that much was never in doubt, and that trite truth, as insistent as a growling stomach, they did not need to learn. But they needed more than "bread alone," and that truth, not as obvious as the hunger, but as real as the possibility of losing their very humanity, they did need to learn. All humans do, perhaps especially we modern ones.

In the course of modernity, we have made our greatest temptation into the chief goal of our lives and the main purpose of our major institutions (i.e., the state, the market, science and technology, and education).[10] Modernity is not just an age in which people believe that "only the world can be the case" (Sloterdijk, 1993, p. 106); more significantly, it is also an age in which *people act as if* only the world were the case, whether or not they believe in transcendent realities.

Most of our social and individual energy and imagination revolves around turning stones into bread. And yet we, both the rich and the poor, are still in the wilderness, plagued by hunger and thirst. For when we live by bread alone, there is never enough bread, not even when we make so much of it that some of it rots away. When we live by bread alone, someone always goes hungry; when we live by bread alone, every bite we take leaves a bitter aftertaste, and the more we eat, the more bitter the taste; when we live by bread alone, we always want more and better bread, as if the bitterness came from the bread itself and not from our living by bread alone. Living by "mundane realities" and for them alone, we remain insatiably restless, and that restlessness in turn contributes to competitiveness, social injustice, and the destruction of the environment. It also constitutes a major obstacle to more just, generous, and caring personal practices and social arrangements.

But why will not bread alone—why will not the unending stream of amazing things and services we create with such incredible ingenuity—still our hunger and keep us delighting? And why would not bread alone still our hunger if we created it righteously and distributed it equitably so that no one is underpaid and the basic needs of all are met? After all, we are material creatures living in a material world, our senses ready for enjoyment.

—∿∿—

---

[10] In the following section I draw on Volf, M. (2016). *Flourishing: Why we need religion in a globalized world*. New Haven, CT: Yale University Press.

Meaning and pleasure belong together. The unity of the two is a source of true joy and a condition of flourishing. No matter what we have and under what conditions we live, we languish when meaning and pleasure are not united. For meaning without pleasure is oppressive, and pleasure without meaning is empty. The separation of meaning and pleasure is a chief defect of our civilization, tied to our stubborn or, perhaps, addiction-induced insistence on living by bread alone. The effects of the separation between meaning and pleasure are felt both in the privacy of our hearts and homes and displayed with vivid destructiveness on the world stage.

There is no meaning—or, perhaps, there are only residues of meaning—in the "bread alone," in things themselves,[11] no matter how complex the way in which they may stimulate our senses. And since there is no meaning in things themselves, there can be no deeper, humanly satisfying pleasure in them either, no deeper enjoyment. Setting reflection on God aside for the moment, let us focus on our experience of ordinary things of life.

Compare two scenes. *Scene one*: I am at home; the night before, I had made a cake following my mother's recipe and using baking and decorating skills I learned from my confectioner father. It is midafternoon, and I am sitting at the old family table with my sister who came for a visit. When we were growing up, on festive occasions we used to sit with our parents around this very table eating the cake, the flourless chocolate cake, made according to that same recipe. The table is set, the candle is lit, the delicacy is on the plate, and I take a bite. I feel pleasure—of sight, of smell, of sound, of taste, of texture, of hunger being satisfied. But the very material act of eating—including those sensations—evokes an entire "world," bringing a flood of explicit and implicit, mental and bodily memories of a happy childhood with a sister I adore. In enjoying the cake, I am relating to my sister, to my parents, to our common customs and our past, to a sense of who I am and hope to remain. The pleasure of these memories and antic-ipations and the pleasure of the physical object overlap, and though I can

---

[11] I use the term "things themselves" not in a technical Kantian sense of "thing in itself" but in a more everyday understanding of "objects" as they are presented to our senses.

distinguish them, I cannot take them apart: to enjoy that cake and to enjoy it in that way *is* to have these memories and anticipations. The cake is a sacrament. The act of eating it is saturated with meaning beyond keeping my soul and body together and giving me physical pleasure.

Scene two: By some miracle, I have found myself in someone's luxury home, alone. In the afternoon, I go to the kitchen and, to my surprise, find in the fridge a piece of flourless chocolate cake. As soon as I see it, I know that it was prepared with more culinary skill than I could ever hope to master; an expert food taster would rate it much higher than my own similar creation. I take a bite and feel pleasure—of sight, of smell, of taste, of texture, of hunger being satisfied, of tasting something uncommonly good (but not of sound, for now the clinking of the fork on the plate seems more a distraction than an enhancement of the experience). And yet, the culinary masterpiece notwithstanding, the pleasure in the second scene is flat compared to the pleasure in the first. You might compare it to the pleasure of a single tone of a single fine instrument played by a fine musician (say, a brief segment of a Bach cello suite in Yo-Yo Ma's rendering) rather than, as in the first scene, the pleasure of an orchestral harmony (say, a movement in Bach's St. John Passion heard as a part of liturgy). Scene one is pleasure with deeper meaning; scene two is pleasure without it.

But it is not just the absence of deeper human meaning that diminishes our pleasures. Twisted modes of meaning do so as well. Consider a third scene, the same as the first one, except that my larger family is gathered around that same old family table, and I dislike the quarrelsome bunch, especially my sister, because in most things, including culinary arts, she is clearly better than I. I am plagued by quiet envy. Making a superior cake according to the heirloom recipe is my attempt to demonstrate to everyone gathered that I am better than—or at least as good as—my sister. Depending on the outcome of the contest into which I have drawn the entire unsuspecting family, even if the cake tasted exactly as good as in the first scene, for me the pleasure of eating it would have been overlaid either by the bitterness of a humiliating defeat or by the saccharine sweetness of a pointless victory which underscores the stupidity of my envy. The pleasure is not monotone; it is orchestral, only the composition is bad, the players are incompetent, and the instruments are out of tune. Pleasure has diminished, even turned into mild pain, not because the cake has undergone a chemical change, but because social discord made it hardly palatable.

All our pleasures are part of a larger structure of meaning, and they derive their ability to satisfy us—indeed, they derive in part their very pleasurableness—from that larger structure of meaning (Bloom, 2010). To desire and pursue things as in themselves sufficient sources of pleasure—to multiply bread or keep creating it with greater culinary sophistication—is to embark upon a futile and often addictive search. To derive pleasure from things placed in the twisted framework of meaning is to twist those pleasures themselves and rob ourselves of the best of them. Either way, the very pleasure we experience lessens our humanity.

The rushing stream of new goods and services modern economies provide—things we often care for more than for anything else in the world—keeps many of us captive to pleasures not worthy of us, a substitute for richer pleasures derived from deeper meaning that eludes us. But our insatiable desire for these goods and services may be more than just a chain of our captivity; it may be a bended knee of longing for deeper satisfaction and richer humanity (Volf, 2010), an unacknowledged *prayer* for the joy of "orchestral harmony" that only the unity of pleasure and genuinely human meaning can bring.[12]

—ᴧᴧᴧ—

For a Christian, the ultimate framework of meaning in which to situate properly every single one of our pleasures, from the very trite to the most

---

[12] Most goods and services in modern economies are designed and sold to satisfy not just physical needs but also powerful psychosocial needs. They mark a group to which a person using them belongs and help define the position he or she holds in the group. You cannot shop for clothes at Walmart and belong to the upper middle class. And if you have a Porsche Cayenne instead of a mere Acura, your standing in the upper middle class will improve; it will give you a competitive advantage in the economy of recognition. Positional goods give satisfaction beyond the enjoyment of things themselves because they have social meaning, but the meaning is shallow and therefore the pleasure is flat. And short-lived.

exquisite ones, is the perception of the world as God's gift. An *abiding experience* of the world as a gift of the God of love would be the single incomparable and all-encompassing pleasure identical with our living itself, a pleasure in which all other pleasures are gathered and united.[13]

To make sense of this claim about love's gift, keep in mind that "gift" is not the object given as such. Little trinkets on the shelves of gift stores are not gifts; they *become* gifts when somebody gives them to somebody else. In other words, gifts are relations.[14] If the world is a gift, then all things to which we relate—and many to which we do not—are also God's relation to us.

Now imagine that you feel a bond to the giver of the gift that is the world, that you "love the LORD your God with all your heart, and with all your soul, and with all your strength, and with all your mind" (Deut. 6:5; Luke 10:27). Imagine also that in response to the God you love, you also "love your neighbor as yourself" (Lev. 19:18; Luke 10:27). Spread wide and boldly the wings of your fancy, and imagine that all your neighbors do the same, which is, of course, exactly how Christians have for centuries imagined the world to come—as the world of love. Each thing in the world is now a relationship marked by love. Each distant star and every gentle touch, each face and every whiff of the freshly plowed earth, in sum, literally every good and beautiful thing shimmers with an aura both vibrantly real and undetectable to our five senses. Each thing in the world is more than itself and just so a source of deep and many-layered pleasure. Love for God and

---

[13] The connection of religious experience to a more complex perception of reality and a deeper enjoyment of it is one of the "commonest entries in conversion records," wrote William James (1902) in his classic *The Varieties of Religious Experience: A Study in Human Nature*. He quoted the following conversion testimony: "Natural objects were glorified, my spiritual vision was so clarified that I saw beauty in every material object in the universe, the woods were vocal with heavenly music" (pp. 243–244). My contention here is that a deepening of one's enjoyment of the world is not simply an aspect of conversion experience, but, since conversion is the beginning of a spiritual journey, a feature of Christian spiritual life as a whole. I offer in the main body of this essay one important reason for such spiritual deepening of enjoyment of the world: A central mark of such spiritual life is an internalized and cultivated perception of the world as God's gift; in conversion this feature of spiritual life comes to a particularly vivid expression.

[14] For an account of gift as relation, see Volf, M. (2005). *Free of charge: Giving and forgiving in a culture stripped of grace.* Grand Rapids, MI: Zondervan.

love for the world are united—from which it follows that the proper love for God will generate both care for and enjoyment of the gift that is the creation. Can those who do not love God enjoy the world and care for it? Of course they can, and many do. The point is that love for God the Creator and lover of creation, rather than undermining care for and enjoyment of things of ordinary life, in fact, underwrites and enhances these.

We cannot save the world; we should not even try. But we can improve the world, not just by creating better goods and services more responsibly and distributing these goods and services more justly among people, but also—and, perhaps, above all—by learning how to rejoice together in the gift that each one of us and the entire world is. That joy will lead to care.

References

Bauman, Z. (1993). *Postmodern ethics*. Oxford, UK: Blackwell.

Bloom, P. (2010). *How pleasure works: The new science of why we like what we like*. New York, NY: W.W. Norton.

Conrad, J. (1990). *Heart of darkness*. New York, NY: Dover Publications. (Original work published 1899)

Fukuyama, F. (1992). *The end of history and the last man*. New York, NY: Free Press.

James, W. (1902). *The varieties of religious experience: A study in human nature*. New York, NY: The Modern Library.

Lukes, S. (1995). *The curious enlightenment of Professor Caritat: A novel of ideas*. London, UK: Verso.

Nietzsche, F. (1995). The utility and liability of history for life (R. T. Gray, Trans.). *The complete works of Friedrich Nietzsche* (Vol. 2, pp. 83–168). Stanford, CA: Stanford University Press.

Rahner, K. (1978). *Foundations of Christian faith* (W. V. Dych, Trans.). New York, NY: Crossroad.

Seneca. (1979). *Ad Lucilium epistulae morales* (R. M. Gummere, Trans.). Cambridge, MA: Harvard University Press. (Original work published circa AD 65)

Sloterdijk, P. (1993). *Weltfremdheit*. Frankfurt, Germany: Suhrkamp Verlag.

Smith, S. B. (2016). *Modernity and its discontents: Making and unmaking the bourgeois from Machiavelli to Bellow*. New Haven, CT: Yale University Press.

Volf, M. (2010). *Captive to the word of God*. Grand Rapids, MI: Eerdmans.

2

MENTORSHIP AS CARE FOR EMERGING ADULTHOOD

A Conversation with Sharon Daloz Parks and
Timothy W. Herrmann

SHARON DALOZ PARKS
Whidbey Institute

TIMOTHY W. HERRMANN
Taylor University

The following exchange represents the second event in a three-part series comprising the 2017 Taylor University Higher Education Symposium. The series theme, *A Calling to Care*, was intended to prompt a conversation about how those in Christian higher education can implement distinct forms of care for college students. This chapter version of the public discussion with Sharon Daloz Parks is offered with the hope that it will stimulate further dialogue about the important topic of caring for students in emerging adulthood, particularly through the development of mentoring environments. In an effort to optimize clarity, content, and flow, the exchange was edited for this publication.

HERRMANN. *The first domain of our conversation is emerging adulthood and mentoring environments. In this session of our symposium we are focusing on "a calling to care," specifically in relationship to college students in their twenty-something decade. What do you consider to be the priorities or key elements in caring for college students?*

PARKS. Thank you for inviting me into this conversation. It may be useful for me to respond to your question first by reflecting for a moment on the word *care*. When I was first invited to come and speak about "a calling to care," two little red flags went up for me. One is that across the years, I have often been aware that when we speak about the importance of mentoring, there are some in the college or university environment across all of American higher education—and especially those (very) overworked people in faculty, staff, or administrative positions—who may immediately think that "care" sounds like "coddling" our students. That perspective holds that students come to college to be grown-ups. So you sent me to the dictionary, where I looked up "care." Sure enough, primary definitions suggest that we "care" for children, for the elderly, and so forth. The word "care" conventionally points toward our response as human beings to the vulnerability of others. My passions have been focused on recognizing that in emerging adulthood, there is an exquisite mix of vulnerability and power. Emerging adults have an emerging strength that is full of life and promise. Thus, if we are caring for students, our sense of care must embrace this more robust sensibility that is not at all sentimental. "Care" doesn't mean coddling. It doesn't mean "mere hand-holding," as "care" is sometimes pejoratively described. So what does it mean to care for our students?

From the dictionary, I moved to another shelf in my library and opened Nel Noddings's (1984) book on caring and ethics. Nel became a professor at Stanford University after an early career teaching mathematics in public schools and then moved into philosophy, ethics, and educational theory. If you do not know her work, I commend it to you. Noddings affirms that we are "created to care," but she also underscores "the courage to care." We have the capacity as human beings to have a feeling for the experience of another and to respond to that—and we sometimes call that the capacity for empathy. Different from sympathy, the experience of empathy moves us to act—to feel with, act with, to act on behalf of. It is closely linked to compassion—to suffer with. That sense of care suggests that we do not so much need to cultivate our capacity to care as we need to reveal our already existing capacity to care. And that may require a kind of courage, for much of what comes at us in today's world defines us as simply self-interested, competitive, greedy, and acquisitive. True, we have all of those capacities, but we also have the capacity to care.

Notably, there is an emerging literature that points toward the clear and urgent significance of this capacity for empathy. Looking at the evolution of our species over time and the challenges looming in our future, Jeremy Rifkin (2009) calls for our becoming an "empathic culture." If we do not, he argues, our species will have trouble surviving on this planet (p. 2). Similarly, George Monbiot (2017) calls for a new political story of empathy and sharing, pointing to a growing recognition that we have survived as a species, in part, because of a somewhat distinctive capacity for mutual aid. There have always been other species that were bigger or more poisonous, but we have a capacity to help each other that is central to who we are, and it is hardwired into us. Thus, we are invited repeatedly, by the very nature of how we have been created, called forth by Creator Spirit continually inviting us to be who we are intended to be—to care.

This is the ground from which we ask, what does it mean to care for emerging adults? Our response is informed, in part, by what we are learning about human development. In the journey of human becoming, we can now reliably discern a series of "stages." I want to underscore, however, that though there are good theoretical warrants for speaking about identifiable and predictable stages of human development, I tend to speak about "eras"—language that does not sound quite as fixed and tidy and thus is less vulnerable to misuse. As one of my colleagues has put it, the usefulness of stage theory is not so much to diagnose or categorize the life of another, but rather to ask: What, now, do we mean to each other? That is, if I can have some understanding of where you are in your developmental journey, and I also have some understanding of where I am, then we can explore who we are and what we can be to each other.

In that spirit, if we are talking about students who are on the cusp of adulthood, we want to be keenly aware of the primary developmental task that marks the threshold of adulthood. Typically—not always, for complex reasons—young adults are ripe for the unfolding of a yet new capacity and strength. That is the development of what we call *critical thought*—the capacity to step outside our own thinking and to wonder: Why do I think that way? This moment in human development is a complicated achievement, and it orients our calling to care for college students. It is a wondrous thing to become aware that if I had grown up in another place, if I had had a different set of experiences, I would bring a different way of seeing, a different way of making meaning, to what is now before me.

The next big realization is that we are all making it up! We are all making meaning, making sense of our experience—and we all do so in somewhat different ways. This means that each of us has an opportunity to see as another might not be able to see, and also that each of us is apt to have blind spots.

We then become curious in new ways. What do we mean by truth? What is true, trustworthy, and dependable—and how do I know? What is my take on reality? What is my way of making sense of the whole of life that is different from the way someone else might view things? That moment is a very significant moment in the journey of faith. We begin to understand faith not as a received set of creedal beliefs, practices, or rituals, but as a verb. "Faith" is something we have, but it is also something we *do* in our ongoing conversation with all of life. This capacity to become conscious of the dynamic meaning-making in which we are all engaged has profound consequences. It is a strength that marks the dawn of the intellectual life and casts us into adulthood in that we become responsible for what we know, think, perceive, believe, honor, take into account, respect, and how we move through the world.

The capacity for critical thought and more mindful action does not automatically take form in us. It is biologically possible to move through our entire adult life without ever developing the capacity for critical thought—always ultimately deferring what and how we "know" to someone else. The formation of critical thought depends, in part, on our having access to contexts that prompt us and require more from us. This is a primary reason for creating colleges and universities—places where critical thought is cultivated and where we learn practices of discernment and more adequate ways of making sense of self, world, and God.

When we do learn to take responsibility for what we know, even at the level of faith, it reorders our relationship to authority and it reorders our sense of power and participation. Thus, much of life is at stake in whether we become fully adult in our capacity for mature faith—a precious and vital possibility.

HERRMANN. *You have spoken so beautifully about caring and have started putting it into the context of a college. We might care individually—for a neighbor, roommate, or friend—however, we might also care communally. You have talked and written a great deal about the idea of mentoring communities. What do you mean by a "mentoring community?"*

PARKS. As I describe more fully in the book *Big Questions, Worthy Dreams* (2011), the formation of critical thought yields a new strength, but also a new vulnerability—the specter of meaninglessness. That is, if everyone is making it up, perhaps nothing is trustworthy and there is no way of achieving a viable grip on reality or a shared sense of significance and possibility. This awareness can lead to depression or to the desire simply to retreat to a less adequate, less mature way of knowing. It is hard to imagine that one can find a place of meaningful commitment within a relativized world—a place where in the midst of radical uncertainty I can still recognize that some ways of making meaning are more worthy and dependable than others.

Classically, what we need in that transition is for Yoda to show up! That transition is the time for Mentor to appear. In classical literature, Mentor is the one whom Odysseus asks to care for his son, Telemachus, while Odysseus goes off to do the terrible things we call war. Mentor is an androgynous figure who presents as male but is the embodiment of Athena—the goddess of wisdom. The mentoring figure has been with us throughout human experience, but it has come into prominence more recently—particularly through the corporate world, and now appears in popular literature. We have not only Yoda but also Gandalf and Dumbledore, along with others. I suspect that this is because as a culture we have a deep knowing that we are in a very profound transitional time. We long for wisdom figures—people who give us confidence that we will make it through this transition. We long for Mentor to show up.

I have become persuaded, however, that in a time of such extraordinary change, it is not enough to have only a one-to-one mentoring relationship—as good and valuable as that can be. We need a mentoring community or a mentoring environment. We are profoundly social creatures, and if we are going to have the courage to create new patterns of life—which is what is now being asked of us—we are going to need the confidence that we will have good company. Our research suggests, and I have come to believe, that if someone looks like they are able to go against the tide in later life, they were probably a part of a mentoring community during their emerging adult years—some "we" that had a shared imagination of what was possible. For example, the early Apple personal computer, the Macintosh, was a rather large box, and inside each one was the signature of every person who had been a part of the group that created it. That group had been given a separate building at Apple, and they had a mentor, Steve Jobs. Together they believed that they were going to change the way the world worked. And they did. My guess is that they are now widely scattered, but each one carries a conviction they are not alone in what they aspire to, what they imagine as possible. It is in this sense that I would wish that every emerging adult could be a part of a mentoring community, a mentoring environment.

HERRMANN. *Would you tell us more about what a mentoring environment looks like, and what care might look like within a mentoring community?*

PARKS. A mentoring community provides the primary five gifts that characterize good mentoring. First is the gift of *recognition*. Mentor sees you. If you look at the figure of Yoda, the biggest features are the eyes and the ears. Mentors know how to see and how to listen. Mentors practice a kind of double vision. They know how to see their protégés both as they are (pretty hard to bluff your mentor) and also as they could become. Mentors see their protégés in a way that the protégés cannot yet see themselves. One mentor said to the protégé, "My job is to stick around until you can see yourself the way I see you." Within mentoring environments you are seen in your particularity, as you are and as you could become.

The second gift is that mentors provide *support*. That can take the form of emotional support, or various kinds of practical support, academic, financial, etc. Sometimes it all gets wrapped up together. All faculty and staff—whether in classrooms or during office hours; counseling, writing, or health centers; residence halls; or administrative offices—have opportunities to provide support. An example: When I flew into Indianapolis last evening, Nick Cartwright, a master's student here at Taylor, drove me to the campus. His employment on campus involves providing logistical support for international students—dealing with travel and visa issues, etc. He was formerly in a position working with students more personally over time. Thinking that he might consider his current position less meaningful in the day-to-day, I asked him if he missed his former job. Significantly, he responded that he believed his current position was equally meaningful because, as an international student himself, he knew what a profound difference it could make in one's college experience to have someone providing the kind of support that he now provides. Another example: A college student named Sue was walking down the hall on her way to her senior seminar. The college president was walking down the hall toward her, and with a casual matter-of-factness pulled a flyer off the wall and said, "Sue, this is for you" (Daloz, Keen, Keen, & Parks, 1996, p. 104). It was an opportunity to teach in a village in Africa. Sue went to Africa and later became an extraordinary international educator.

That last example is what I call a mentoring moment—not necessarily a long-term relationship, but a moment when somebody sees and makes a connection between a protégé and their potential. I experienced a mentoring moment when I was deciding whether or not to take up doctoral studies. I was in my thirties, attending a conference, entering a hotel, walking through a revolving door with a woman whom I knew by reputation to be a respected professor. I said, "I'm thinking about getting a doctorate and wondering if I should." She responded, "It is a terrible thing to have to go through, but we need more women to do it." We parted ways on the other side of the door. But it was a very important moment in my discernment, apart from which I might not be sitting here today having this conversation. Mentoring moments are ones in which we are seen and responded to in some way that takes up residence inside us and provides vital support in the ongoing motion of life.

Third, mentors do a very fancy two-step. They not only provide support, they also offer rightly timed challenge. If we are underchallenged, we are bored. If we are overchallenged, we are stressed and become vulnerable to giving up. Given an array of puzzles, we will tend to choose one that is just a little bit harder than the one we already know how to solve. So rightly timed challenge is an artful feature of mentoring environments. It might be a seemingly small step or a big leap—the question is whether it is within our energies to take it on. We may be challenged within a discipline of study, or challenged to take on a new contemplative practice, or to take up a competitive sport, or to modify our behavior, or to expand our horizons, or to develop a new cognitive or emotional skill. We may be challenged to consider issues of injustice. We may be challenged to stretch our spiritual understanding. The invitation to step up to the stretch of mind, heart, and soul that is integral to mentoring relationships is often precipitated by the ways in which mentoring environments artfully pose big-enough questions.

A good deal of mentoring literature could be summed up in these three gifts: *recognition, support, challenge.* But I would add two more. Thus, fourth, mentors *inspire.* Mentors may challenge one's capacities in the present, but they also inspire worthy dreams of a possible future—a fitting imagination of one's adulthood. Mentors instill a sense of aspiration that is worthy of the particular promise of one's life. In our society—in every society—there are default settings for who we might become. The default settings do not necessarily serve to truly inspire, "in-spirit." If they are not aligned with the currents of Spirit that move within us, among us, and beyond us, they may not bring to fulfillment the promise of our lives.

Mentors inspire in many ways, but two are useful to note here. Sometimes the mentoring environment or a mentor as a person may lead an exemplary and inspiring life—embodying a worthy imagination of what the protégé too could become. But sometimes, and particularly in our times, a mentor points beyond where the mentor has yet been able to go. George Bernard Shaw is quoted as saying, "I'm not a teacher: only a fellow traveler of whom you asked the way. I pointed ahead—ahead of myself as well as you." Today we are all standing on new moral and ethical frontiers, with questions that our species has never previously had to entertain. So while mentoring is, indeed, sometimes hierarchical in terms of age or position, our times call us to a considerable amount of shoulder-to-shoulder mentoring. As we are called into unprecedented landscapes, a mentor may play a role in inspiring future possibilities, but the mentor and protégé together will share the puzzle of discovering how to best proceed.

This brings us to the fifth gift of mentors and mentoring communities. Mentoring environments are *accountable*. I mean this in several ways, but the grounding element here is that the mentor does not exploit the protégé. If I am a member of the faculty advising freshman students, it is unlikely that every student I work with is a perfect fit for the major I happen to teach. This brings us full circle to the gift of seeing each student in his or her particularity and recognizing his or her own emergent potential and calling. I must not exploit the promise of a student's life. This form of exploitation happens particularly in grad school—in doctoral programs, for example, when a notably talented student is co-opted into a professor's research lab and abandons the question, born of his or her own curiosity and calling, that brought him or her to graduate school in the first place. There are additional forms of exploitation to which protégés are also vulnerable—sexual, political, emotional, financial—all of which must be avoided since the role of mentor includes protecting the emerging adult.

Mentors are also accountable in another way. Good mentors, like good parents, know how to hold on, let go, and stick around. By "hold on," I mean, for example, how William G. Perry, who was an extraordinary director of a counseling center at Harvard, would work with a student. Sometimes the student would come to a point in the counseling process when he or she would reveal something that the student felt to be deeply shameful. Then if the student didn't show up for the following session, rather than rigidly honoring the protocols—it is up to the student, and if they don't want to come back, that is their business—Bill would think, "Hmmm . . . I need to get out my butterfly net." Then he would "happen" to cross paths with that student on campus, and he would just warmly smile and say, "Hello, good to see you," and continue on his way. Often the student would then be able to return to the healing work. It takes a kind of exquisite skill simply to hold the hope when the protégé is vulnerable to despair.

Knowing how to "let go" is equally important. There is a considerable amount of lore and literature about the perils of mentor-protégé relationships gone bad. Mentors often and understandably need the protégé as much as the protégé needs the mentor, but everyone should be able to outgrow their mentor. Part of being accountable as a mentor is to let go with grace.

Though protégés may move away into their own competence and calling, mentors need to know how "to stick around"—to be available. We have found that former protégés sometimes want to come back and just check in—and there can be goodness and meaning in that. Sometimes in later life, there is a desire to check in with a mentoring community, such as when alums return to campus. Or one may want to reconnect with a professor or member of the staff or administration who made a difference, to let them know that they mattered, to express gratitude. And I think also that sometimes the protégé returns, in part, because there is an inchoate longing to be seen again, as one was seen before. We never fully outgrow that. That gift is another part of what a mentor, a mentoring environment, or a mentoring community can provide within the arc of a lifetime.

HERRMANN. *If modeling is part of mentoring, then seeing your investment in these ideas and beliefs and hearing how they motivate you provides a powerful lesson for us who are here today. Thank you.*

We are now moving to our second domain, contemporary conditions that impact mentoring. You have talked about the importance of mentoring in every generation. So while mentoring isn't something we are just discovering, are there ways in which our current social and political landscapes affect how mentoring does or doesn't occur?

PARKS. It is really quite ironic that when the mentor is appearing as a significant figure in popular literature, at the same time, the practice of mentoring is being eroded in our cultural life. I first began to discover this in conversation with young adults who chose to go into law. Traditionally, a law firm was a very natural mentoring environment. The younger lawyers were learning from the older lawyers, and that dynamic was an integral part of becoming a lawyer. Too often now, the experience of a new young lawyer in the firm is that the older lawyers are not available for the kinds of conversations that we might assume would be organically built into the system. That is, as our business model increasingly bleeds into every other sector of our society, two lawyers talking with each other is not a billable hour. So, if both senior and junior lawyers are under pressure to achieve their billable hours, talking to each other is a "waste of time." Similarly, when our economic models place efficiency as the highest value, then it may be seen as efficient to fire fifty-year-olds, who cost more, and hire the twenty-somethings for less, who will not only be thrilled to have a job, but may even be grateful for an unpaid internship. This kind of dynamic pits one generation against the other, and older generations may withhold their capacity for mentoring because, while recognizing the potential of the younger generation, they perceive it as a threat rather than an invitation to a significant and even vital relationship.

An aspect of this disturbance in the cogwheeling of the generations is, as we all recognize, the digital or tech divide. Digital natives can be frustrated by older folks' lack of ease (or interest) in tech, and older ones can feel that the world is changing at such a fast clip that perhaps they have nothing relevant to offer anyway. Moreover, the generations are also segmented into differing markets, again set at odds with each other. These factors are real.

They mask, but they do not erase the reality of the distinctive potential and vulnerability of emerging adults who appropriately are dependent upon access to mentors and mentoring environments for the fulfillment of the promise of their lives.

Further, it is not too much to say that the strength and viability of a culture as it moves into the future similarly depends upon the art and practice of mentoring communities. I become angry and sorrowful when people in my generation say, "We have made a mess of things, so the next generation will have to figure it out." Alternatively, the call to shoulder-to-shoulder mentoring is the deeper truth because the generations need each other, as together we create and care for the future. When we reflectively pay attention, we discover that there are conversations we share, particularly if we take up the big-enough questions posed by the unprecedented challenges of our time.

HERRMANN. *As an avowed Luddite, I must ask you: Would it be fair to characterize what you have said as communicating that modern electronic technology is at the root of most of our problems [asked as a joke]?*

PARKS. No, I'm not quite willing to go there. Our new communications technologies are both a blessing and a challenge—playing a big role in shaping the frontiers we now face. Thus, one of our biggest questions is, "How are we as a species going to evolve in right relationship to both our technologies and to our natural environment?" I live in the Seattle area, and when I pose this question there I ask: "How are we going to evolve in right relationship to both the salmon and the microchip?" (Yes, someone asked if I was reducing it all to a matter of fish and chips!) The question is how do we imagine ourselves into the future? Now that we can place microchips inside our bodies and play with the genome, we must grapple with very big questions about not only the personal question, "Who am I?" but also collectively with the questions, "What does it mean to be a human being?" and "Who do we want to become?"

HERRMANN. *Thank you. You have given a wonderfully thoughtful response to a rather frivolous question. Going back to your law firm example, it seems to me that we are often more careful in accounting for financial cost than human cost. How can we convince higher educational leaders that the investment in mentoring and mentoring communities makes sense? Are there reasons college leaders should view this as an important institutional interest?*

PARKS. Part of our work is to recognize that we "care" when we realize that another is linked to our possibility, and we all have a stake in the intelligence and character of the next generation. Another part of our work is to recognize the limitations of our current economic imagination. Human beings have created many differing economic systems throughout our history, and we are at a moment when we need a new economic imagination, a reordering of the meta-narratives we all live by. One of the biggest questions I am personally feeling called to work on is, "What is the new narrative, particularly for the United States, that will serve us in a way that is truly worthy as we move into the future?" Will we compose a narrative that is faithful and truthful about our past, including our strengths, our aspirations, our sins, and our sorrows? What kind of narrative is worthy of the promise of human life and the life of our planet? Thus, part of our shared work now is about how we are going to develop a more adequate response to the question: What story are we in? This is ultimately and intimately a question of faith. It is a theological question. It is a religious question. It is an economic question. In the life of our current society, we are a divided people within a cacophony of stories. As a nation and as a global people, we need a shared story that appropriately honors our particular stories and at the same time conveys that *we are all in this together.*

HERRMANN. *We could spend a long time on that point, but let's address a related question: the formation of faith and the role of religion in emerging adulthood. In* Big Questions, Worthy Dreams *(2011), you wrote, "The promise and vulnerability of emerging adulthood lie in the experience of the birth of critical awareness and consequently in the dissolution and recomposition of the meaning of self, other, world, and 'God'" (p. 8). Could you talk a little bit about this process of dissolution and recomposition, and particularly the opportunities and vulnerabilities it presents?*

PARKS. Earlier we spoke about the composing mind and how as human beings we are continually making meaning. In our early years, it is very appropriate that what I ultimately trust is what I've been told by (hopefully trustworthy) authority figures in my life. We would wish for everyone that they would grow up in a context where they are given good story, where they are given good religion, where they have a received faith—and where there are practices by which each generation conveys to the next the best by which it has come to live. Then, as one moves into adulthood, each generation must explore and test that which has been received, even the most "sacred truths." A part of becoming adult is asking whether what I have received is true and worthy, and do the words and rituals that hold it convey the same meaning as in the past, or does it need to be translated into new forms? Sometimes that process is prompted by academic study and sometimes it is prompted by personal life experience—or a combination of both.

A story I tell in *Big Questions, Worthy Dreams* is that when I was just beginning to teach in the college context, I was honored to be invited to teach in a team-taught course. It was required of all freshmen. I realized that one of the students in my section of the course didn't think it was a great honor to take this course. So in my "best caring mode," I invited him to stay after class. I had an agenda, which was that by the time we finished talking, he was going to understand what a privilege it was to take this class. We began to talk. I assumed that overall he was doing well. He was an athlete and he had an older brother on campus, an athlete in another sport who helped pave the way for him. But then my student began to talk about how he wasn't so sure he was "a football player" or if that was an identity made up by his high school newspaper. He then told me about his parents' divorce that had happened within the past couple of years. He concluded by looking at me boldly and asking: "Do you know what it is like to have lost everything you ever really loved?"

We didn't get around to talking about the class that day. But I was glad I could look back and say to him that I knew something about that. My parents were not divorced, and I made my way through college reasonably well. But in my graduate school years, I did undergo a loss that pretty much shattered my sense of how I thought life would always work. At the time, I wouldn't have said that I experienced the loss of God, but God was silent. We are helped to think about that kind of experience by Richard R. Niebuhr, with whom I studied at Harvard Divinity School. He writes about the journey of faith, using the metaphors of *shipwreck*, *gladness*, and *amazement*. He uses *shipwreck* to refer to those experiences of the dissolution of how we thought life worked, or how it would always be. Then if we do wash up on a new shore of insight and understanding, what we feel is *gladness*. He describes this gladness as "an intellectual affection," because what we experience is a new kind of knowing. Then Niebuhr adds the word *amazement*, because we are amazed that this could happen and we have survived. When our faith—our earlier form of making meaning—was lost, we didn't know that it was possible to discover a larger, more adequate faith on the other side of that loss. It has been said that Passover and Easter are what happens to us when we look back and say, "I survived that?!"

I am offended by any piety that glibly intones that those kinds of experiences are good for us because they build character. None of us wants character that badly. But I would not want to go back to a time when I didn't know what I know now. The maturing of faith, however, does not require everyone to undergo a dramatic shipwreck experience. I recall one young woman who said, "The loss of my earlier faith was sort of like watching a slowly declining stock—it just kept drifting down and eventually faded away without any big crashing moment, but it was over."

So it is critical that you ask if there are real perils in this process. The primary peril is that on the one hand, there are some who are never invited to a more mature faith, and on the other hand, there are others who develop critical thought but do not wash up on a new and good shore. You will recall that I spoke earlier of the possibility not only of new meaning, but also the discovery of meaninglessness. Faith becomes mature when it can have a doubt of itself. But doubt also can lead to despair. A guy I knew in college married my roommate and was headed to medical school. When we were all about twenty-eight, he committed suicide. It wasn't a suicide that was inevitable. It didn't have to happen. There were, indeed, severe stresses in his life, and some of them were related to our arrangements around medical school education. This is why it matters so much that we are present to each other and care for each other personally and institutionally. We can't be careless about this journey of human development, and here—especially in the era of the emerging adult years—so much is at stake. If we fail to meet the moment, the casualties—not only in the form of suicides—are manifold: the potential contributions to society that are never realized when emerging adults are not recognized, supported, and challenged; the young black and Hispanic men who are only offered prison as a "mentoring environment," who learn how to survive but not how to genuinely thrive; the number of premature marriages that are formed in someone's failure to offer access to a more worthy dream; the number of lives who choose the path of business or tech, not because they are following a calling, but simply because they are subject to parental expectations or to the default settings du jour. There is a very long list of the ways that the distinctive gifts of a particular life—and thousands of lives—can be lost to the human story forever if we do not care, if we are not accountable, if we fail to craft the mentoring communities—in the classroom, in the residence hall, in the lab, on the playing field, within the off-campus project, and in the college or university as a whole—that appropriately and powerfully recognize the vulnerability and nurture the promise of the emerging adult years.

HERRMANN. Thank you so much for your thoughtful comments; it has been so good to hear from you today.

As I have been listening, I have been thinking that one of the marks of a good speaker or teacher is that their listeners find themselves wanting to do something—or perhaps even "be something" different in the future. I have certainly experienced this today, and I suspect that this room is filled with other people who feel likewise. So again, we want to thank you for being here with us, for thinking deeply about these important issues, and for sharing so beautifully. We are truly grateful for the way that you have honored us today, but even more, we are grateful for the way that you have served emerging adults throughout your career. Again, thank you.

References

Daloz, L. A. P., Keen, C. H., Keen, J. P., & Parks, S. D. (1996). *Common fire: Leading lives of commitment in a complex world.* Boston, MA: Beacon Press.

Monbiot, G. (2017). *Out of the wreckage: A new politics for an age of crisis.* Brooklyn, NY: Verso.

Noddings, N. (1984). *Caring: A feminine approach to ethics & moral education.* Berkeley and Los Angeles, CA: University of California Press.

Parks, S. D. (2011). *Big questions, worthy dreams: Mentoring emerging adults in their search for meaning, purpose, and faith.* Revised 10th Anniversary Edition. San Francisco, CA: Jossey-Bass.

Rifkin, J. (2009). *The empathic civilization: The race to global consciousness in a world of crisis.* New York, NY: Jeremy P. Tarcher/Penguin.

3

NEL NODDINGS'S ETHIC OF CARE

Thoughts for Student Development Educators

KELLY A. YORDY

Taylor University

It is no surprise to higher education practitioners that these are trying times in our industry. A casual perusal of news and current events reveals the state of U.S. colleges and universities as a volatile one, and the enterprise collectively finds itself in an increasingly deteriorating environment (Altbach, 2016; Schuster & Finkelstein, 2007). According to Altbach (2016), "Financial cutbacks, enrollment uncertainties, pressures for accountability, and confusion about academic goals are among the challenges facing American colleges and universities in the early twenty-first century" (p. 84). With no shortage of pressing issues confronting the academy, it is imperative for scholars and practitioners to maintain focus on the primary purpose of higher education: student learning and success (Keeling, 2014).

It is with this firmly anchored focal point that I delve into the central theme of this chapter: the necessity for an ethic of care in higher education and, more specifically, in the realm of student development. Given the urgent concerns vying for the academy's attention, the skepticism of key stakeholders and the general public is warranted. To some extent, it is understandable why higher education's critics would question an educator's focus on caring for students beyond their academic education or basic needs when seemingly more exigent necessities have surfaced throughout the academy in recent years. Indeed, some would even argue the current generation of college students is fragile and overly self-focused, requiring "tough love" instead of deeper care. However, regardless of one's approval or critique of the millennial generation, "higher education can be vital space for the exploration and learning that is the heart and essence of the twenty-something decade and a preferred institution for the formation of adulthood" (Parks, 2011, p. 203). Thus, college student educators have the unique privilege, opportunity, and responsibility to come alongside students on the journey to adulthood. This chapter seeks to answer not only the question of *why* but more critically *how* to care for college students by first delving into the ethic of care theory. The importance of an ethic of care in higher education will follow. Finally, the theory of care ethics will be discussed in the context of Christian practitioners serving in the field of student development.

The Ethic of Care

The concept of an ethic of care was first introduced by Carol Gilligan (1982) in her book *In a Different Voice: Psychological Theory and Women's Development* as a critical response to Kohlberg's (1981) theory of moral development. The first of Gilligan's two primary critiques of Kohlberg's theory was its basis in research conducted solely on adolescent boys. Her second critique was Kohlberg's conclusion that women were unable to reach the same level of moral development as their male counterparts (Patton, Renn, Guido, & Quaye, 2016). To refute Kohlberg's claim, Gilligan (1982) conducted her own research and concluded,

> The reiterative use by the women of the words *selfish* and
> *responsible* in talking about moral conflict and choice, given the

underlying moral orientation that this language reflects, sets the
women apart from the men whom Kohlberg studied and points
toward a different understanding of moral development. (p. 73)

Based on Gilligan's research, the early theorists and critics of the ethic of care
initially identified it as a form of feminist or feminine ethics (Monchinski,
2010). Although the ethic of care theory may have found its nascent stages
of development occurring in the realm of feminist ethics, it has long since
evolved into a theory applicable to both genders and inclusive of mascu-
line and feminine ethics. As a prominent early theorist of care ethics, Nel
Noddings (1984, 2016) advanced the conversation to include the field of
education. Before exploring the benefits of care ethics in higher education, however, it is first beneficial to provide an overview of the ethic of
care theory.

What Is an Ethic of Care?

The construct of caring possesses an array of meanings, particularly in light
of the wide variety of factions and professions that exist within society.
The ways in which a medical professional exhibits care for her patients
will differ from the care a teacher offers his students and certainly from
the care mothers and fathers provide their children. Still, there are certain generalizable aspects to the caring construct. While the dictionary
provides a plethora of definitions for care and caring, Noddings (1984)
posited, "One cares for something or someone if one has a regard for
or inclination toward that something or someone" (p. 9). This definition
may provide a helpful—albeit superficial—foundation from which to start.
However, using this definition of care, I may, for example, care for a good
book similarly to how I care for my neighbor. Thus, in moving toward
a deeper understanding of care, Noddings explained, "Caring involves
stepping out of one's own personal frame of reference into the other's. . . .
Our attention, our mental engrossment, is on the cared-for, not on ourselves" (p. 24). With this more meaningful definition, Noddings began to
convey the necessity of shifting the carer's focus and attention away from

oneself and onto the cared-for. Noddings further expounded, "To act as one-caring, then, is to act with special regard for the particular person in a concrete situation" (p. 24).

Stated alternatively, "to act with special regard" could simply indicate that a caring relationship is established between the cared-for and the carer. Both Gilligan (1982) and Noddings (1984) argued that caring relationships are the foundation of care ethics, in that caring relationships are based on the needs and concerns of the individual. Caring relationships are inherent to human beings (Keeling, 2014), and while they are exhibited in varying degrees throughout humanity, at their cores, "relationship[s] require connection[s]" (Gilligan, 1993, p. xix). Indeed, we are "hard-wired for connection" (Keeling, 2014, p. 142). Monchinski (2010) concurred: "From the perspective of an ethic of care, relationships between human beings are not optional; they are primary" (p. 56). It is this connection, this foundation of caring relationships, on which we base our understanding of care ethics.

Natural Caring vs. Ethical Caring

In order to fully grasp the ethic of care concept, it is helpful to juxtapose ethical caring with natural caring. By expanding upon Gilligan's (1982) concept, Noddings (1984) created a dichotomy between natural caring and ethical caring. Natural caring, according to Noddings, occurs when one acts on behalf of the other simply because he or she desires to do so. A common example Noddings used to describe natural caring is a mother caring for her child. While the universality of the motherhood model of natural care has been criticized (Clement, 1996; Monchinski, 2010), it is nevertheless helpful in understanding the difference between natural and ethical caring. To further explain natural caring, Noddings (2016) offered,

> Anyone who lives beyond infancy has at least an inkling of
> having been cared for; that inkling may not be enough to really
> understand what it means to be cared for, and certainly it is

often inadequate to produce a fully caring adult. But it is the
root of our responsibility to one another. At least in part because
of this rootedness in care, in many common human situations,
we respond spontaneously to another's plight. (p. 225)

Natural caring, therefore, is innate; it is instinctive, spontaneous, and is
not considered by the carer to be an obligation or to require ethical effort.

Ethical caring, in contrast, "does have to be summoned" (Noddings,
2016, p. 226), and it is not spontaneous. According to Noddings, "An inner
voice grumbles, 'I ought but I don't want to'" (p. 226). She continued, "On
these occasions, we need not turn to a principle; more effectively, we turn
to our memories of caring and being cared for and a picture or ideal of
ourselves as carers" (p. 226). While the distinction between natural and
ethical caring provides a helpful framework, at this point a Christian's
beliefs will likely diverge from Noddings's philosophy. As unpacked in the
biblical critique offered later in this chapter, what motivates a Christian's
ethical caring does not need to primarily arise from one's memories of
caring or being cared for, or a potentially egocentric desire to see oneself
in an ideal light. Additionally, it is imperative to note that while Noddings
contrasted natural and ethical caring, the implications of each should not
result in false dichotomies. While natural caring arises instinctively, it is
not always easy, and ethical caring is not always hard. Similarly, it would
be misleading to imply that natural caring is always carried out cheerfully,
while ethical caring always occurs begrudgingly.

Since Gilligan's (1982) and Noddings's (1984) early work, the ethic of
care theory has been debated, modified, and further developed, and it is
not without controversy. However, as Manning, Kinzie, and Schuh (2006)
contended, "The impact of this early work cannot be underestimated. Its
influence on the student affairs field, a field marked by care and connection, has been significant" (p. 101). Before delving into the benefits of an
ethic of care in the field of student development, however, it is important
first to consider an ethic of care in the broader academic milieu.

The Ethic of Care in the Higher Education Context

The emphasis on caring relationships thus far has focused on the connection between two people: the carer and the cared-for. In the context of higher education, however, the relationship between the student and the institution is worth examining. Unfortunately, this relationship is typically not understood or viewed as one of equals (Keeling, 2014). This reality is especially true if the institution is perceived as inanimate and devoid of the ability to care for the student. As Keeling maintained, "That relationship, if acknowledged at all, is usually defined through rules, traditions, and customs, not by mutual understanding, responsiveness, or empathy" (p. 142). This is a lamentable perception, considering the term *alma mater*—which refers to the college or university one attended—means "fostering mother" (Rhatigan, 2013). In truth, colleges and universities are comprised of people—faculty and staff who care for individual students on behalf of the institution. Thus, the institution's (the carer's) ability to care for the student (the cared-for) depends almost completely on the ability and willingness (e.g., time or mental and emotional capacity) of individual faculty and staff members to exhibit an ethic of care with students.

Historically, institutions of higher education have espoused a deeply-rooted dedication to the education, success, and well-being of their students. The colonial colleges, though arguably authoritarian in nature, exhibited a comprehensive level of care for the earliest college students. According to Rhatigan (2013), "One could say that the 'ethic of caring' evident in the colonial college was present in every phase of a student's life" (p. 206), although "this was not the warm and fuzzy caring behavior one would imagine today" (p. 206). In recent years, however, broadly speaking the commitment to the care and development of students may have begun to wane. According to Dalton and Crosby (2013), "Administrators and faculty have greatly ascended in importance in the academy, while students have diminished markedly in priority and focus" (p. 197). The general public has noticed this shift in the academy as well (Manning et al., 2006). As Dalton and Crosby argued, "Colleges and universities have come under considerable criticism for their disregard of students' welfare, especially the holistic well-being of undergraduate students" (p. 197). While modern-day college educators have come a long way in their methods of care for students, the priority of comprehensive care exhibited by colonial college educators could be considered a great strength of the early American higher education system—and may now be deteriorating into a substantial weakness.

In addition to what appears to be a philosophical shift in academia's commitment to students' education and well-being, pragmatic realities such as financial cutbacks have resulted in the now commonplace practice of replacing retired tenured faculty with part-time and adjunct instructors (Altbach, 2016; Eagan, Jaeger, & Grantham, 2015; Gerber, 2014). Although this change is only one of the many effects of the financial crisis, the deprofessionalization of U.S. faculty is having a severe impact on college students. According to Eagan et al. (2015), part-time instructors "are less available to students, interact with students less frequently, and spend less time preparing for courses. . . . they are significantly less likely to use student-centered teaching methods, which have been linked to student success and retention" (p. 453). Essentially, fewer faculty and staff members are willing or able to provide the care necessary to educate and develop students. While this abating priority, focus on, or dedication to students may not be surprising considering the aforementioned pressures facing the academy, it is troublesome. These are difficult realities; however, the benefits of embracing an ethic of care model can provide student development educators and other personnel throughout the institution with valuable tools to care for students.

The Ethic of Care Philosophy

Despite trends of diminishing dedication to students in the larger higher education context, many curricular and cocurricular educators continue to place students at the center of their work. All educators who care about students are dedicated not only to the education of the whole person but also are responsible for representing students' issues and needs to the broader institution. In this way, the implication of an ethic of care obligates educators—and colleges and universities as a whole—to consider the policies, practices, and actions that affect students' whole-person education. As Dalton and Crosby (2013) maintained, "Institutions that promote an ethic of care create environments of hospitality for students" (p. 202). While it may be most apparent to consider an ethic of care on the personal, individual level of interacting with students, it is imperative for educators not to overlook an ethic of care at the macro level of the institution.

Macro levels of care. Most higher education practitioners and graduate students preparing for similar roles did not enter the field for the purpose of developing or revising institutional policies. Typically, those working in the field had a transformational college experience—often by virtue of a professor, mentor, or student development practitioner—and want to similarly educate and care for students as a vocation. Nevertheless, it is critical for student development educators to recognize how their commitment to providing leadership in implementing and revising the policies and practices of the institution is an essential form of caring for students as well.

While student development educators are responsible for providing guidance at the macro level in areas not typically familiar to practitioners whose responsibilities and training occurred in non-student-centric fields, an ethic of care will not exist without purposeful dedication on the part of the institution. According to Keeling (2014),

> An ethic of care requires that colleges and universities recognize, acknowledge, and manage or overcome individual, community, and systematic challenges and barriers to students' well-being. . . . this obligation must be understood, accepted, and discharged at a systemic and institutional level, as opposed to being addressed randomly through purely personal and individual commitments and actions. (p. 146)

As Keeling explained, the systematic, macro-level approach to an ethic of care is critical to successfully meeting the needs of students and educating the whole person. Once institutional support for an ethic of care is evident at the macro level, it is beneficial to next explore an ethic of care at the micro level.

Micro levels of care. Although Dalton and Crosby (2013) supported utilizing an ethic of care model for students and acknowledged the institution's "obligation to consider each student holistically, including intellectual, emotional, physical, social, and ethical aspects" (p. 201), they recognized the practical necessity to care for students through "active involvement in the context of students' lives" (p. 201). This active involvement requires educators to engage in relational care with students at the individual level. Rabin and Smith (2013) maintained,

> [While] we can *care about* those we do not know well, we can *care for* only those with whom we have built relationships. To care for requires the carer to understand the needs of another. To care for students, teachers need to know their students well enough to understand their unique motivations and needs. (p. 165)

But what exactly does it mean to *know* students, and what are the implications of knowing the students on our campuses? Addressing this issue theologically, Garber (2014) suggested,

> If we were to take Hebrew scripture, from Genesis to Malachi, listening to and learning the way that knowledge is understood, it would come to something like this: *to have knowledge of* means *to have responsibility to* means *to have care for*. If one knows, then one cares; if one does not care, then one does not know. (p. 100)

Thus, even a narrow understanding and knowledge of students' educational and developmental needs ethically requires responsibility, and in turn, should engender care. However, this knowledge of and care for our students need not be carried out in a perfunctory manner. On the contrary, according to Palmer (1993), "A knowledge that springs from love . . . will wrap the knower and the known in compassion, in a bond of awesome responsibility as well as transforming joy; it will call us to involvement, mutuality, and accountability" (p. 9). Ultimately, institutions, faculty, staff, and administrators can easily *care about* the students they admit into their institutions on a superficial level. But truly and authentically *caring for* students is only possible through knowing and establishing caring relationships with students.

Strike (1999) supported this concept through juxtaposing justice and caring:

> Justice insists on general rules. It has a concept of the self that
> reduces everyone to a thin moral sameness and that denigrates
> the importance of the particularities and relationships. Caring,
> in contrast, is context sensitive, has a situated self, and is funda-
> mentally concerned for relationships. (p. 22)

Furthermore, in order to form relationships with students, the carers must engage in a process of engrossment. The term *engrossment*, however, "is not meant to suggest infatuation, obsession, or single-mindedness" (Noddings, 2016, p. 231). According to Rabin and Smith (2013), engrossment is necessary "to enable one to go from caring about to caring for, and the challenge of building relationships that enable that leap" (p. 171). Nelsen (2013) further suggested that "Engrossment describes the complex process in which the [carer] brackets self-interests and anticipated interpretations of what the cared-for wants or needs and remains open to the cared-for's needs and interests" (p. 352). Nelsen's and Noddings's (2016) views are congruent in that an ethic of care is not a spontaneous outflow like natural care, but rather it is deliberate and intentional:

> A process of inquiry must be at work because determining how
> to respond to a particular other within a caring relation does
> not just appear to the carer during the state of engrossment. The
> carer must somehow determine how to respond and how to

enhance the moral relation, a process that entails some form of *relational* inquiry. (Nelsen, 2013, p. 353)

If genuinely caring for students necessitates an intentional, relational inquiry into the needs and interests of the students, how can institutions better equip their educators to provide an ethic of care to students? Many perspectives pertinent to the holistic development of college students with accompanying advice for educators sound great in theory but fall short in practical application. Similarly, the ethic of care concept can easily fall into this category without thoughtful understanding and application of Noddings's (2016) four components of care in education: modeling, dialogue, practice, and confirmation.

Modeling. In modeling care, Noddings (2016) suggested, "We are mainly concerned with the growth of our students as carers and cared-fors. We have to show in our own behavior what it means to care . . . we demonstrate our caring in our relations with them" (p. 230). Noddings was quick to point out, however, that our motives for caring for our students are not so that we can model how to care. Instead, through genuinely caring for our students, modeling will be the natural by-product.

Dialogue. In addition to modeling what it means to care, we must engage students in dialogue about caring. "Dialogue is implied by the phenomenology of caring. When we care, we receive the other in an open and genuine way" (Noddings, 2016, p. 231). Most student development practitioners have experienced shepherding a student through an institution's disciplinary process—and most have also encountered the student's frustration and opposition when he or she realizes the repercussions of his or her actions. In an effort to utilize the disciplinary process to facilitate character development in students, student development practitioners can exhibit an ethic of care by entering into open, honest, and genuine dialogue with students. Because dialogue is such an integral contribution to the growth of students (Noddings, 2016), it is an essential element of caring relationships between students and educators in higher education.

Practice. Noddings (2016) suggested, "The experiences in which we immerse ourselves tend to produce a 'mentality'" (p. 232). Essentially, if our aim as educators is to holistically develop students, then we must practice entering into caring relationships with students in a way that cultivates this value. Noddings also advocated practical experiences that will help produce students who genuinely care for one another. Regardless of whether these experiences are curricular, cocurricular, or a combination of the two, opportunities for self-reflection within those experiences are a necessary component in the development of care.

Confirmation. As the final component to caring ethics, the act of confirmation encourages and affirms positive development in students:

> When we confirm someone, we identify a better self and
> encourage its development. To do this, we must know the other
> reasonably well. Otherwise, we cannot see what the other is
> really striving for, what ideal he or she may long to make real.
> (Noddings, 2016, p. 232)

Thus, we again consider the importance of knowledge and relationship in educating and developing students. In addition, trust and continuity are requirements for confirmation (Noddings, 2016). Continuity is needed to acquire knowledge of the student and to assist in building credibility and trust. Because trust and continuity are required elements of confirmation, Noddings recommended that educators and students remain together for several years if possible. On smaller college campuses, this longevity is perhaps more feasible. Because academic faculty members often teach multiple courses for freshmen through seniors, students attending smaller colleges are likely to interact with the same professors from one year to the next. Additionally, smaller college campuses offer more students the opportunity to interact to a greater extent with student development educators through extracurricular activities and leadership positions as well as in their residence halls. Perhaps student development educators should consider how they might remain in caring relationships with students for consecutive years to maximize opportunities for students' education and development.

Strengths of the Ethic of Care Philosophy

Because a discussion of the strengths of the ethic of care philosophy could constitute its own chapter, I will highlight only the most substantial. First and foremost, an ethic of care provides an exceptional level of service to students. As Manning et al. (2006) explained, this form of "student service" is not a model that prioritizes bureaucracy, procedure, and administrative pragmatism. Instead, the ethic of care philosophy provides service to students by emphasizing "the ability of the student affairs educator to devote time to students in need, assist the student in the most sensitive and compassionate means possible, and create a climate in which every member of the community is valued" (p. 102). Of course, institutions of higher education should universally prioritize student success. At times, however, the institution may be motivated by factors other than the well-being of the student. National rankings, increased retention and graduation rates, satisfying students and parents as consumers, and hopes that satisfied alumni will translate to financial donors may all contribute to the emphasis on student success. Whether an institution's motivations for student success are genuine or not, "allegiance to the goal of student success has steered many college and universities toward behaviors that approximate the application of an ethic of care" (Keeling, 2014, p. 145). Ideally, colleges and universities will prioritize the education and development of their students and recognize the substantial benefits the ethic of care philosophy can provide. While institutions may accrue benefit from caring for students, this must be understood as a by-product and not be the motivator for adhering to an ethic of care.

The environment fostered by the ethic of care model is another strength. This culture of care permeates the campus community as student development educators gain a reputation of trustworthiness (Manning et al., 2006). In a caring environment, "students obtain the emotional support necessary to form healthy relationships, engage in constructive risk taking, and pursue developmental tasks that lead to engagement and involvement" (p. 102). As student development educators create and implement services and programs through the ethic of care model, ideally "safety nets are established, and fewer students fall through the cracks. These initiatives are even more effective when student and academic affairs collaborate on these efforts" (p. 102). The benefits to the institution may prove to be numerous when a culture of care is established throughout the campus community.

One of the most important benefits of nurturing a culture of care is the increased potential for learning. Indeed, "Promoting an ethic of care enhances the well-being of students and encourages a powerful learning environment for them" (Dalton & Crosby, 2013, p. 202). Dalton and Crosby maintained that, when students are connected to their campus communities, they are prone to investing more deeply in their academic pursuits. In their research exploring the faculty-student interaction, Fleming, Purnell, and Wang (2013) discovered that caring relationships between students and faculty actually develop the caring self in students. Thus, exhibiting an ethic of care is not only beneficial to the individual student, but it perpetuates as the student then "pays it forward" by replicating this in care for others. Taken one step further, we begin to comprehend the reciprocal potential of an ethic of care in education: as an institutional environment of care encourages students' deeper investment in their academics, a caring relationship exhibited in the classroom likewise strengthens the campus community's culture of care.

In her book *The New Better Off*, Courtney Martin (2016) suggested, "While we can't expect anything important in life to be easy or entirely enjoyable, we also shouldn't buy into the tired public narrative that work is inherently dehumanizing or boring or pointless" (p. 28). It is unlikely that college student educators view their work in this way—as "just a job." Certainly, what motivated us to pursue this work was not the high pay or an easy, compact workweek schedule (think middle-of-the-night hospital runs, late-night student leader meetings, and weekend hall events). Instead, student development educators typically pursue this work because it is deeply satisfying. While the ethic of care philosophy may seem natural in the context of student development work, the urgent needs of today—or what we believe are the urgent needs of today—can often supersede what is most important in our daily work until we lose sight of why we entered this field to begin with. Suddenly, the very aspects of our work that originally called us to this field have taken a back seat to the daily pressures and bureaucracies of higher education. In this way, an important strength of the ethic of care philosophy is its ability to refocus our priorities. Of course, there are certain realities to every job that do not fall under the category of "deeply meaningful." But when weeks have passed since we can remember tasks or conversations that exhibited care for students, it is necessary to consider the ways in which we might use the ethic of care philosophy to refocus our work to become more beneficial to students and more satisfying to us as educators.

Weaknesses of the Ethic of Care Model

One of the chief criticisms of higher education is its continuously rising costs. State appropriations and government funding have decreased in recent years, and institutions are shouldering the financial burdens of unfunded mandates. The growing consumer mindset of students and their parents has pressured institutions to meet their demands, leaving many colleges and universities in a state of significant financial stress. In light of these fiscal concerns, it is important to acknowledge that the ethic of care philosophy is incredibly time-consuming and thus creates an expensive culture in which to function. In addition to the aforementioned budget constraints, because of the "increased psychological and emotional needs of students and the sheer volume of student affairs work growing each year" (Manning et al., 2006, p. 102), the labor-intensive nature of the practices required to facilitate an ethic of care may be of concern.

The ethic of care philosophy is not only time-consuming but is also quite difficult to codify and assess and thus may be difficult to justify in the current climate of higher education. With a never-ending cycle of ideas and proposals competing for limited resources, supporting educators in creating a culture of caring for students without a clear and concrete connection to institutional priorities may be a difficult sell. However, it is the right thing to do and clearly honors the best traditions of higher education. If an institution can commit to allowing its faculty and staff the time and space needed to employ an ethic of care in their work with students, the benefits the institution will receive in return will surely justify the investments.

One of the major weakness of the ethic of care philosophy that must be addressed is the possibility of caring for students in an unhealthy, paternalistic manner. Student development educators are not students' parents and must be cautious not to personify *in loco parentis* in a way that compromises their work or, more importantly, hinders the development and education of students. As Manning et al. (2006) warned, "Any professional using this model must be vigilant so that the care does not turn into coddling" (p. 103). The college experience should provide emerging adults with opportunities to exhibit independence and develop as individuals away from their parents. For this reason, it is important not to care for students in a manner that removes critical challenges, thus impeding their personal growth and development. While there are risks to consider, the benefits of the ethic of care model far outweigh the potential weaknesses.

Demonstrating an Ethic of Care as Christians in Student Development

In a preceding section of this chapter, I briefly mentioned my critique of Noddings's (2016) recommendation that, for ethical caring motivation, "we turn to our memories of caring and being cared for and a picture or ideal of ourselves as carers" (p. 226). As Christian scholars and practitioners in higher education, we have the advantage of intimately knowing the One who has created in us the ability to care for others. Though at times we may feel natural care for our students, often our care is offered "in obedience" because we know it is the right thing—the loving thing—to do. Ordinarily, the care we demonstrate to our students will be ethical (i.e., deliberate, intentional, and at times obligatory) as opposed to natural (i.e., innate, instinctive, and spontaneous). It is also true that, as educators, the act of caring for our students may engender memories of being cared for by our former mentors and educators; however, these memories need not be the sole source of fuel for our ability to care.

As Christians, our love and care for others should not reflect a legalistic attitude, and we should not expect anything in return. Indeed, we will do more for our fellow humans out of love than we would out of obligation. Thus, while we typically demonstrate ethical care instead of natural care to our students, the source of care can and should be love, not obligation. Certainly, the word *love* in this context could merely denote one's affection toward another; and yet, biblically, this word elicits a much richer understanding of love. Jesus told his disciples, "As the Father has loved me, so have I loved you" (John 15:9). He continued, "My command is this: Love each other as I have loved you" (John 15:12). In this way, God's love for Jesus and his love for us enable us to love and care for one another.

Although the wellspring of our care for students is the gracious love we receive from God, part of the gift of God's love allows for the opportunity—indeed, the necessity—to simultaneously care for ourselves while we care for others. The ethic of care philosophy not only permits but also actually insists that carers preserve their capacity to care by caring for themselves concurrently. As Monchinski (2010) explained, "An ethic of care has been misconstrued to be 'other-directed' at the expense of the self. . . . Care should not be seen as synonymous with servitude and subordination of the self to others" (p. 62). Not only is this point critical to the health and wellness of the carer, but ultimately, "failing to care for the self detracts from the care we can provide others" (p. 62). Although Jesus's love and care for us is synonymous with "servitude and subordination of the self," culminating in the ultimate act of love and sacrifice on the cross, we are not perfect as he is—our capacity to care is finite. In order to care well for our students, we must first be effective stewards in caring for ourselves.

Attention to issues of self-care, rest, and solitude is already vast and continuously expanding. It is beyond the scope of this chapter to delve into the numerous meaningful ways in which student development educators can and should care for themselves. However, it is worth briefly examining Jesus's actions, as he remains our constant example. Throughout the Gospels, Jesus withdrew from his disciples (his primary "cared-fors") for rest and solitude. In one example, "Very early in the morning, while it was still dark, Jesus got up, left the house and went off to a solitary place, where he prayed" (Mark 1:35). Jesus used times of solitude to pray and be with God. We care for ourselves by doing the same, which may include intentional times of prayer and solitude with God, observing Sabbath, exploring God's creation, calling a friend, listening to music, or simply playing with our children. Essentially, we care for ourselves by enjoying the fullness of what God has provided for us to experience—and in doing so, we enhance our capacity to ethically care for our students.

Final Thoughts

This chapter has focused on the ethic of care philosophy in the higher education context, particularly as a way for Christian student development educators to approach their sacred work with college students. An overview of Nel Noddings's ethic of care was offered, as well as specific ways institutions and individual educators might implement caring ethics on their campuses. I hope the ideas humbly offered in this chapter inspire reflection, refinement, and encouragement to you in your work. Indeed, the process of formulating these thoughts has granted me the opportunity to reflect on my own work in higher education and the ways in which I succeed and fail at caring for students. What a comfort it is to know "we are God's masterpiece. He has created us anew in Christ Jesus, so we can do the good things he planned for us long ago" (Eph. 2:10 NLT).

Times of worship often end with a benediction—a blessing. If you will allow me to consider this work as an act of worship, I would like to conclude by sharing two blessings that have brought meaning to my own work. First, in a poem by John O'Donohue (2008) called "For Work," O'Donohue considers the sacredness of work as a source of renewal to oneself and those with whom one works. I encourage you to read the poem and allow O'Donohue's words to ruminate as you consider your own work as "wellsprings of refreshment, inspiration, and excitement" (O'Donohue, 2008, p. 146).

And finally, I pray the following Scriptures will bless you as you continue to cultivate and offer daily acts of worship to our Lord:

May you experience the love of Christ, though it is too great to understand fully. Then you will be made complete with all the fullness of life and power that comes from God. Now all glory to God, who is able, through his mighty power at work within us, to accomplish infinitely more than we might ask or think. Glory to him in the church and in Christ Jesus through all generations forever and ever! Amen. (Eph. 3:19–21 NLT)

References

Altbach, P. G. (2016). Harsh realities: The professoriate in the twenty-first century. In M. Bastedo, P. Altbach, & P. J. Gumport (Eds.), *American higher education in the twenty-first century* (4th ed., pp. 84–109). Baltimore, MD: Johns Hopkins University Press.

Clement, G. (1996). *Care, autonomy, and justice: Feminism and the ethic of care.* Boulder, CO: Westview Press.

Dalton, J. C., & Crosby, P. C. (2013). Second-class citizens on campus? Promoting an ethic of care for undergraduates in student-college relationships. *Journal of College and Character, 14*, 197–204. doi:10.1515/jcc-2013–0026

Eagan, M. K., Jaeger, A., & Grantham, A. (2015). Supporting the academic majority: Policies and practices related to part-time faculty's job satisfaction. *The Journal of Higher Education, 86*, 449–480. doi:10.1080/00221546.2015.1177371

Fleming, J. L., Purnell, J., & Wang, Y. (2013). Student-faculty interaction and the development of an ethic of care. In A. R. Rockenbach & M. J. Mayhew (Eds.), *Spirituality in college students' lives: Translating research into practice* (pp. 153–169). New York, NY: Routledge.

Garber, S. (2014). *Visions of vocation: Common grace for the common good.* Downers Grove, IL: InterVarsity Press.

Gerber, L. (2014). *The rise and decline of faculty governance: Professionalization and the modern American university.* Baltimore, MD: Johns Hopkins University Press.

Gilligan, C. (1982). *In a different voice: Psychological theory and women's development.* Cambridge, MA: Harvard University Press.

Gilligan, C. (1993). Letter to readers, 1993. In C. Gilligan, *In a different voice: Psychological theory and women's development* (pp. ix–xxvii). Cambridge, MA: Harvard University Press.

Keeling, R. P. (2014). An ethic of care in higher education: Well-being and learning. *Journal of College and Character, 15*, 141–148. doi:10.1515/jcc-2014-0018

Kohlberg, L. (1981). *Essays on moral development: Vol. I. The philosophy of moral development.* San Francisco, CA: Harper & Row.

Manning, K., Kinzie, J., & Schuh, J. (2006). *One size does not fit all: Traditional and innovative models of student affairs practice.* New York, NY: Routledge.

Martin, C. E. (2016). *The new better off: Reinventing the American dream.* Berkeley, CA: Seal Press.

Monchinski, T. (2010). *Education in hope: Critical pedagogies and the ethic of care.* New York, NY: Peter Lang.

Nelsen, P. (2013). The inquiry of care. *Educational Theory, 63*, 351–368. doi:10.1111/edth.12028

Noddings, N. (1984). *Caring: A feminine approach to ethics and moral education.* Berkeley, CA: University of California Press.

Noddings, N. (2016). *Philosophy of education.* Boulder, CO: Westview Press.

O'Donohue, J. (2008). *To bless the space between us: A book of blessings.* New York, NY: Doubleday.

Palmer, P. J. (1993). *To know as we are known: Education as a spiritual journey.* New York, NY: HarperCollins Publishers.

Parks, S. D. (2011). *Big questions, worthy dreams: Mentoring emerging adults in their search for meaning, purpose, and faith.* San Francisco, CA: Jossey-Bass.

Patton, L. D., Renn, K. A., Guido, F. M., & Quaye, S. J. (2016). *Student development in college: Theory, research, and practice* (3rd ed.). San Francisco, CA: Jossey-Bass.

Rabin, C., & Smith, G. (2013). Teaching care ethics: Conceptual understandings and stories for learning. *Journal of Moral Education, 42*, 164–176. doi:10.1080/03057240.2013.785942

Rhatigan, J. (2013). The enduring value of an ethic of caring. *Journal of College and Character, 14*, 205–212. doi:10.1515/jcc-2013-0027

Schuster, J. H., & Finkelstein, M. J. (2007). *On the brink: Assessing the status of the American faculty.* Retrieved from the Center for Studies in Higher Education at the University of California-Berkeley website: https://cshe.berkeley.edu/sites/default/files/publications/rop.schuster.3.07.pdf

Strike, K. A. (1999). *Justice, caring, and universality: In defense of moral pluralism.* In M. Katz, N. Noddings, & K. Strike (Eds.), *Justice and caring* (pp. 21–36). New York, NY: Teachers College Press.

4

TEACHING STUDENTS TO CARE FOR THEMSELVES

KIRSTEN D. RIEDEL
Belmont University

EMILIE K. HOFFMAN
Taylor University

JESSICA L. MARTIN
Taylor University

In a culture where phrases like "treat yo self," "binge-watching Netflix," and "you do you" are pervasive across college and university campuses, it is evident students value—and are making significant attempts toward—taking care of themselves. In this pursuit, students do not have to look any further than their phones for a multitude of blog posts, Pinterest pins, BuzzFeed articles, and various posts on social media that highlight the importance of self-care and provide ideas for its implementation. Such consistent messages—while helpful in many ways—also perpetuate students' individualistic and fragile views of themselves, creating in them an almost frantic sense of urgency about prioritizing self-care. In this regard, the self-care students often implement tends to be reactive in nature, and therefore can easily become self-indulgent.

Crisis of College Student Care

Research on coping mechanisms among college students has consistently found that emotional and avoidance coping strategies are common (Brougham, Zail, Mendoza, & Miller, 2009; Dwyer & Cummings, 2001; Dyson & Renk, 2006). Such studies also show these coping strategies are frequently associated with greater levels of stress, anxiety, and depression (Dyson & Renk, 2006; Sasaki & Yamasaki, 2007; Soderstrom, Dolbier, Leiferman, & Steinhardt, 2000). Consequently, while students might believe their self-care habits are beneficial to their well-being, such habits often, in reality, exacerbate the challenges they face.

Perhaps the most prominent example of this reality is college students' widespread use of smartphones and social media. Jean Twenge's (2017) influential research on students in the "iGeneration" highlighted the detrimental impact of smartphones on today's teens—many of whom are in college. In her article "Have Smartphones Destroyed a Generation?," Twenge argued, "It's not an exaggeration to describe iGen as being on the brink of the worst mental-health crisis in decades. Much of this deterioration can be traced to their phones" (para. 10). More specifically, Twenge found that "teens who spend more time than average on screens are more likely to be unhappy" (para. 26) and are more likely "to report symptoms of depression" (para. 31). She also noted that many teens sleep less than is recommended, possibly due to late-night and early-morning smartphone use—which is increasingly problematic since people who do not get sufficient sleep are "prone to depression and anxiety" (para. 44). Even twenty years ago, before smartphones existed, Kraut et al. (1998) described the "Internet paradox," positing that frequent use of technologies negatively impacts psychological well-being since it produces the same kind of loneliness, isolation, and depression that using the Internet was originally intended to relieve.

Without intervention, college students will continue perpetuating their susceptibility to anxiety and depression through the exact strategies and mediums employed for the purpose of self-care. The irony of this phenomenon creates the impetus for this chapter. Educators across college and university campuses have the increasingly critical responsibility of responding to this crisis of care by providing the care students *actually* need. This calling invites educators to care for students by teaching students to care for themselves.

Self-Care Defined

Self-care is defined in the literature as "maintaining a healthy and balanced lifestyle through individually determined activities" (Jeffries, Spagna, & Behring, 2017, para. 1). Accordingly, self-care practices are described as "self-initiated activities . . . and include healthy eating, sleeping, exercising, and socializing behaviors" (Moses, Bradley, & O'Callaghan, 2016). Jeffries et al. (2017) reminded us that such practices have been found "to improve productivity and a sense of well-being as well as physical and emotional health in a variety of . . . settings" (para. 1). However, while appropriate self-care evidently contributes to more healthy, productive, and successful people, the aforementioned definitions and practices are insufficient without an end toward which they are employed.

A Theology of Self-Care

James K. A. Smith (2009), in his book *Desiring the Kingdom*, argued that humans are fundamentally desiring creatures and that our desires—or our loves—are formed by our practices. Smith described the influence of such practices—which he refers to as liturgies—in our lives. He wrote, "The motions and rhythms of embodied routines train our minds and hearts so that we develop habits—sort of attitudinal reflexes—that make us tend to act in certain ways toward certain ends" (p. 59). Keeping Smith's work in mind, it is imperative that educators teach college students to care for themselves by assisting them in the development of self-care liturgies that shape their loves toward the ultimate end of God and his kingdom. With pursuit of such ends, habits of self-care are no longer viewed as indulgent, avoidant, or productivity-focused. Rather, self-care becomes an essential and formative practice in faithfulness to God that has the restorative effect of addressing the brokenness present in all and which is at the root of much of what needs "fixing."

Scripture reinforces the importance of caring for oneself and offers an end toward which self-care practices ought to be employed, specifically highlighting the primary call in the Gospels to love God and love neighbor "with all your heart and with all your soul and with all your mind" (Matt. 22:37). In order to faithfully love God with our whole selves, we must practice good stewardship of our hearts, souls, and minds—essentially, our entire created being.

Gates (2015) described this calling to love God and love our neighbor as ourselves (as commanded in Mark 12:31), explaining that just as we are not to indulge others but to care for them, so we ought not to indulge ourselves but to care for ourselves. We care for ourselves faithfully by first recognizing that doing so honors God; next distinguishing between self-care and self-indulgence; then viewing love for God, others, and ourselves as intricately connected; and eventually becoming less self-indulgent and more loving. From a clearly Christian perspective Gates contended,

> Self-care is not indulging ourselves without regard for God and others, but recognizing our legitimate need to care for ourselves by seeking what ultimately benefits us and protecting ourselves from what ultimately harms us—even as we do the same for God and others. (p. 17)

Stott (1984) further explained that this vision of care calls us to recognize that our embodied selves are a result of both the Creation and the Fall. Consequently, faithful self-care practices ought to only value, affirm, and strengthen our created selves—or "everything in us that is compatible with Jesus Christ" (p. 28).

Finally, perhaps the greatest inspiration for self-care from a theological perspective comes from Christ's example in Scripture. Throughout the Gospels, Jesus frequently withdrew to be alone with God and to pray—despite the persistent demands placed upon him (Luke 5:15–16). Henri Nouwen (1995) described the importance of this practice, writing that the place where we are alone with God on the mountaintop is where we "listen to the voice of the One who calls [us] the beloved" (para. 13). He continued,

"Jesus listened to that voice all the time, and he was able to walk right through life" (para. 15). Nouwen later explained this place is where we must start in order to eventually move into community and then into ministry. Jesus's habit of embracing solitude, therefore, serves as the perfect model toward which to orient our practices of self-care.

A Renewed Vision for College Student Self-Care

This theological framework of practicing self-care with the purpose of pursuing God and his kingdom has noteworthy implications for Christian educators hoping to teach students to care for themselves. With recognition of this theological framework as well as the previously mentioned current crisis of student care, the purpose of the discussion that follows is to advocate a renewed vision for college student self-care. Educators ought to practice good stewardship by urging students to consider—and ultimately, embody—three critical characteristics of self-care. First, self-care is intentional and rhythmic; it is a *practice*. Second, self-care requires *mindfulness* of both the self and the practice. And third, self-care is *holistic*. While this discussion will address four realms of self-care independently, there are many natural connections between them, and the understanding of this integration is vital for implementing holistic self-care. Thus, the content that follows will provide research on self-care as well as a theology for caring for the whole self—the physical, emotional, intellectual, and spiritual aspects of self that comprise our created beings.

Caring for the Physical Self

According to the most recent American College Health Association's (2017) National College Health Assessment of undergraduate students, 84 percent of college students describe their general health as good, very good, or excellent. In the same survey, however, only 3.6 percent of the students eat five or more fruits and vegetables per day, and 50 percent meet the recommendations for moderate-intensity exercise, vigorous-intensity exercise, or a combination of the two. Students' daily fruit and vegetable consumption as well as daily physical activity progressively decrease from the first to the seventh semester (Butler, Black, Blue, & Gretebeck, 2004; Crombie, Ilich, Dutton, Panton, & Abood, 2009; Ferrara, 2009; Nelson, Lust, Story, & Ehlinger, 2008; Small, Bailey-Davis, Morgan, & Maggs, 2013). Students are motivated to engage in exercise in order to look physically fit, improve their personal appearance, manage their weight, and reduce stress (English, 2009; Pauline, 2013).

A major concern across these studies is the long-term impact of health behaviors—or the lack of healthy lifestyle choices—that are established in college and follow individuals into adulthood (Buckworth & Nigg, 2004; Sparling & Snow, 2002; U.S. National Center for Health Statistics, 2012). While these studies have focused on broader healthy behaviors, the consistent lack of caring for one's physical self is concerning (Ashcraft & Gatto, 2015; Stark, Hoekstra, Hazel, & Barton, 2012). Students' perception of their health appears disconnected from appropriate lifestyle behaviors, and their motivation is often superficial and appearance-driven. Overwhelmingly, these studies challenge universities as well as individual educators to address diet and exercise intervention with college students (English, 2009; Huang et al., 2003; Katz, Davis, & Findlay, 2002; Keating, Guan, Piñero, & Bridges, 2005; Nelson et al., 2008; Sparling & Snow, 2002).

As many of these studies highlight, college students' physical health—from eating patterns to physical activity levels, stress, and sleep patterns—is not optimal (Katz et al., 2002). The primary reasons for addressing the physical health of college students, according to the research, are grounded in medical and public health concerns (U.S. National Center for Health Statistics, 2012). Promoting physical exercise and nutrition is important to preventing illnesses and other health issues. Yet is that the only reason for teaching students to care for the physical self?

A Theology of Physical Self-Care

The Christian conception of humanity is fundamentally embodied. Throughout Scripture, the value of the body is highlighted. Beginning in Genesis, God as Creator forms the body and breathes in life (Gen. 2:7). The incarnation of Jesus Christ—God himself—is also significant. Paul wrote about "the redemption of our bodies" (Rom. 8:23), and the book of Revelation paints a picture of the future kingdom in which the body will not be discarded. Rather, the body will be redeemed and become a part of the new creation. While it is not yet fully known how wholly redeemed human bodies will function, the risen Christ and his existence in human flesh convey the significance of the embodied life.

The biblical account of humanity addresses one's physical nature. As 1 Corinthians 6:19 reminds us, "Do you not know that your bodies are temples of the Holy Spirit, who is in you?" Further, this account of human nature suggests the various aspects of humanity are deeply interrelated. In other words, the diverse dimensions of one's life—physical, emotional, intellectual, and spiritual—are interdependent. One's physical life impacts and interacts with one's spiritual, intellectual, and emotional experiences. This conclusion is not to suggest, however, that physical health is a mere demonstration of a pre-existing spiritual health, but rather that physical health and life partially shape one's spiritual condition. The motivation for Christians to care for their physical selves should be rooted in the Christian account of human flourishing and God's intention to redeem the fullness of human life.

Teaching Students to Care for the Physical Self

The state of college students' physical health varies from individual to individual—for reasons ranging from preventive measures through exercise and diet to managing acute symptoms or chronic conditions. While student development educators are not physicians or health experts, they do have a responsibility to encourage and support college students in caring appropriately for their physical bodies. The goal is not for all students to achieve a particular state of physical health. Rather, educators address the physical realm not only recognizing its impact on other areas of one's life, but also motivated as Christians to care for the body through the lens of stewardship. Most educators have a sense of general health recommendations—whether exercising for thirty minutes three times per week, eating five servings of fruits and vegetables daily, sleeping six to eight hours per night, or seeing a doctor annually. At times, such suggestions can become another task one *should* be doing or an area where one is lacking. How do we inculcate physical self-care practices in students that are appropriate to their circumstances and individual needs?

Meet students where they are. The majority of college students (87 percent) describe being "overwhelmed by all they need to do" in the assessment by the American College Health Association (2017). Especially for high-achieving or people-pleasing students, asking if they are caring for their physical health may serve as a stressor. Instead, find a way to listen to what the student already senses in her or his life.

Check motives and increase awareness. As already mentioned, physical health motivation for many college students is driven by physical appearance (Keating et al., 2005). While exercising, eating well, and caring for one's physical health contributes to positive views of self, it also lends itself to performance-driven behavior or negative coping strategies like disordered eating and stress (Katz et al., 2002; Pauline, 2013). When approaching conversations on physical self-care, carefully hold in tension the benefits of physical self-care while helping students grow in awareness of the impact of physical health on their lives.

Assess current habits. One specific method for developing such awareness could be helping students assess the habits already present in their lives. Do they stress-eat while studying or to stay awake? What are their sleep routines? If they have chronic conditions, are they regularly seeing their doctor, and how are they managing symptoms? What other areas of their lives take precedence, and why might that be the case? The academic calendar has periods of high workload, and some healthy habits may take a back seat during those stretches. Do students return to healthy habits once an assignment or exam has passed?

Navigate the process slowly. If students identify steps toward physical self-care, challenge them to pace themselves in that process. Habits and rhythms are formed over time, and not every area they may want to change is necessary or feasible, depending on the situation and other factors. Therefore, it is imperative to help students continuously reflect on what they are doing and why they are doing it. Caring for one's physical health is not merely about controlling, pushing, or striving. Instead, it is about better understanding the embodied self and learning how to better live in the manner in which God created us.

Caring for the Emotional Self

According to neuroscientist and physician Antonio Damasio (1994), "Emotions are not a luxury. They play a role in communicating meaning to others, and may also play a cognitive guidance role" (p. 130). Damasio further explained, "Feelings have a say on how the rest of the brain and cognition go about their business. Their influence is immense . . . Feelings are a powerful influence on reason" (p. 160). Emotional well-being is one of the most recognizable and talked-about components of the larger self-care conversation, yet mental health issues continue to rise on university campuses. A 2015–2016 survey by the Association for University and College Counseling Center Directors found that 57.1 percent of directors reported an increase in the severity of student mental health concerns and related behavior on their campuses (Reetz, Bershad, LeViness, & Whitlock, 2016). Considering this disconnect, how do we reframe the conversation on emotional self-care in a way that acknowledges the significance of emotion to the whole self?

In reframing the conversation, recognizing that emotional self-care is only a small portion of the larger mental health conversation is important. Educators must know the limitations of their own expertise in matters of mental health. Since referral often represents the greatest act of care an educator can offer, knowing and working closely with campus mental health practitioners should free educators to enter into conversations about caring for the emotional self without fear of being ill-equipped to navigate more serious mental health concerns.

A Theology of Emotional Self-Care

As Christian educators, we ought to be mindful of the tremendous responsibility of guiding students well in matters of emotional self-care. Therefore, a brief theology of emotion is helpful in framing a context for rightly considering emotion. Benner (1984) pointed out that Scripture is full of instances where God and his people act in and reveal emotion. Such examples affirm our emotionality by speaking through and to our emotions rather than just our intellect. Failing to appropriately acknowledge emotion as an integral component of the self means renouncing significant aspects of faith and possibly even religion itself. To this end, Puritan Jonathan Edwards (1821) made his appeal in *Treatise Concerning Religious Affections*:

> For although to true religion there must indeed be something
> else besides affection, yet true religion consists so much in the
> affections that there could be no true religion without them . . .
> If the great things of religion are rightly understood, they will
> affect the heart . . . God has given to mankind affections, for the
> same purpose as that for which he has given all the faculties
> and principles of the human soul, [namely] that they might
> be subservient to man's chief end, and the great business for
> which God has created him, that is, the business of religion.
> (pp. 44–47)

Edwards also cautioned, "there are false affections, and there are true . . . The right way is not to reject all affections, nor to approve all; but to distinguish between affections, approving some and rejecting others; separating between the wheat and the chaff" (p. 46). In simpler terms, Edwards gave a charge to manage emotions well to the end mentioned above.

Teaching Students to Care for the Emotional Self

The need for emotional self-care is apparent in the anxiety-ridden lives of many college students. What information proves helpful to educators seeking to come alongside students in the daily endeavor to care for the emotional self? Without crossing the boundaries of formal counseling, how might educators help their students understand and manage emotions as a means of caring for self?

Emotional intelligence. Modern psychology has posed emotional intelligence (EI) as a framework for measuring how people regulate emotions, providing opportunities for more effective and healthy management. Therefore, research concerning EI is far-reaching in its implications for mindful emotional self-care. Salovey and Mayer (1990)—foundational EI researchers—concluded, "The person with emotional intelligence can be thought of as having attained at least a limited form of positive mental health . . . awareness often lead[s] to the effective regulation of affect within themselves and others, and so contributes to well-being" (p. 201). Though many models of emotional intelligence appear in the literature, the model proposed by Salovey and Mayer, and later expanded upon by Salovey and Grewal (2005), is the most widely accepted by the scientific community. Salovey and Mayer (1990) formally defined EI as "the ability to monitor one's own and others' feelings, to discriminate among them, and to use this information to guide one's thinking and action" (p. 189).

Salovey and Grewal (2005) later broke down the definition into four primary abilities: perceiving emotions, using emotions, understanding emotions, and managing emotions. While perceiving emotions involves the "ability to detect and decipher emotions," using emotions involves the "ability to harness emotions to facilitate various cognitive activities, such as thinking and problem solving" (p. 281). Understanding emotion is the "ability to comprehend emotion language and to appreciate complicated relationships among emotions" (p. 281). Lastly, managing emotions is the "ability to regulate emotions in both ourselves and in others" (p. 282).

Social support. The relationship between EI and supportive social networks is implicit in the literature (Salovey & Grewal, 2005; Zeidner, Matthews, & Roberts, 2009). More specifically, the relationship is cyclical in nature: higher EI is predictive of richer and more satisfying relationships, and supportive social networks prove necessary in developing EI (Zeidner et al., 2009). Social interactions within supportive networks allow students opportunities to see appropriate emotions and emotional responses mod-eled. As EI increases, students learn to appropriately manage and disclose emotions in ways that in turn contribute to richer relationships, and thus to increased life satisfaction (Extremera & Fernández-Berrocal, 2006).

Recently, Brené Brown's research and resulting TED Talks have gar-nered much attention, prompting an increased conversation concerning the power of emotions—like shame—in defining relationships and self-worth, and vice versa. Brown has repeatedly pointed out how shame can lead to a variety of maladaptive tendencies when left unchecked. Brown (2012b) argued that shame—growing in secrecy, silence, and judg-ment—is combated by empathy, expressed within supportive relation-ships. However, the most powerful form of empathy stems from authentic human connection, which requires vulnerability. In her book *Daring Greatly,* Brown (2012a) explained, "Vulnerability is the birthplace of love, belonging, joy, courage, empathy, and creativity. It is the source of hope, empathy, accountability, and authenticity" (p. 34). Social connectedness is then a predictor of resilience—the ability to adaptively cope with neg-ative emotions, states, and the situations that trigger them (Capanna et al., 2013).

Practically speaking, students can build and practice EI—independently and then within community—by naming emotions as they emerge, reflect-ing on emotion-triggering situations and consequent responses, speaking positively of themselves when dialoguing with others, and inviting per-spectives and feedback from others. In doing so, students practice skills in all four of Salovey and Grewal's (2005) previously defined EI abilities. Educators can help foster emotional intelligence in students by encouraging and facilitating engagement in supportive communities. By engaging in these supportive systems, practitioners can effectively model, promote, and celebrate appropriate emotional expression. Considering the importance of emotion to a student's general well-being and sense of self, Christian educators should take care not to shy away from conversations concerning emotion. Further, educators should seek to express the highest levels of empathy when faced with self-disclosing students.

Caring for the Intellectual Self

A holistic view of self necessitates consideration of the intellectual dimension in addition to the physical and emotional dimensions outlined previously. The National Wellness Institute (1976) described this intellectual dimension as the one that "recognizes one's creative, stimulating mental activities" (p. 1). In a variety of learning environments across college and university campuses, the importance of nurturing the intellectual self is implicitly communicated, but educators must also recognize their responsibility to emphasize this importance through more explicit messages—by inviting students to consider themselves as intellectual beings and to prioritize the practice of caring for themselves in this area.

The National Wellness Institute (1976) highlighted the value of students receiving such support, that when utilizing human and learning resources from the university and outside communities, "a well person cherishes intellectual growth and stimulation" (p. 2). Carr and Claxton (2002) similarly described the purpose of such educational efforts as shifting toward "a concern with the development of aptitudes and attitudes that will equip young people to function well under conditions of complexity, uncertainty, and individual responsibility: to help them become, in other words, good real-life learners" (p. 9). This compelling vision creates the impetus for further exploring the idea of caring for the intellectual self.

A Theology of Intellectual Self-Care

The role of Christian educators also emphasizes the value of teaching students to care for their intellectual selves, making these conversations an opportunity for practicing good stewardship. Willie Jennings (2015) made a theological case for caring for the mind:

> Christian intellectual life is by no means the sole property of
> those who inhabit the theological academy or those who live
> their lives from the sight lines of pulpits or the comfort of coun-
> selor chairs. Christian intellectual life is the inheritance of every
> Christian and the calling on every believer to reflect deeply

about their faith from the sites in this world that matter—where lives are at stake, and hope hangs in the balance. (para. 1)

Scripture affirms this calling, as Paul urged us to offer up our entire bodies as a "living sacrifice, holy and pleasing to God," and to be "transformed by the renewing of your mind" (Rom. 12:1–2). Caring for the mind—or the intellectual self—is, therefore, a worthy and necessary endeavor toward the end of Christian flourishing.

Furthermore, in *Educating for Shalom*, Nicholas Wolterstorff (2004) argued that learning, and specifically Christian learning, is an essential pursuit—especially toward the Christian call to seek shalom, or human flourishing. In adopting a posture of learning for shalom, what then must educators challenge students to learn in order to practice self-care for their intellect?

Teaching Students to Care for the Intellectual Self

Perhaps of most immediate concern in this learning process is reminding students of their responsibility to actively participate in the intellectual aspects of their educational journey. While this responsibility may seem obvious to us as educators, students can easily view their education as a product to be consumed rather than an experience in which to fully engage. Furthermore, college students can be inclined to give less attention to their intellectual selves with an assumption that this aspect of the self is naturally attended to in an academic environment. The following components of intellectual self-care are thus offered as specific aspects of the learning process for which students ought to take ownership.

Critical thinking. Halpern (1999) defined critical thinking as referring to "the use of cognitive skills or strategies that increase the probability of a desirable outcome. Critical thinking is purposeful, reasoned, and goal-directed" (p. 70). Barnett (2015) added that critical thinking involves responding to "questions that cannot be answered definitively" (para. 3) and "values inquiry, ongoing questioning of one's assumptions, recognition of the need to know in order to think, and openness to new ideas" (para. 3). Given the complexity of critical thinking as a concept and a practice, developing critical thinking as a means of caring for self requires students to exert significant effort. Such effort is also needed for students to recognize why and how to apply their critical thinking (Halpern, 1999). Over time, "students learn to value the process of learning, inquiry, and critical self-reflection while acquiring and constructing self-knowledge" (Rusche & Jason, 2011, p. 338).

Metacognition. "Metacognition, or thinking about one's thinking, is key to facilitating lasting learning experiences and developing lifelong learners" (DePaul University Teaching Commons, 2017). Metacognition is frequently conceptualized as having two primary components: knowledge and self-regulation (Kuhn & Dean, 2004; Pintrich, 2002; Sperling, Howard, Staley, & DuBois, 2004; Tanner, 2012). The first component of metacognition refers to having knowledge of strategies for thinking and learning, while the second component refers to monitoring cognitive tasks and knowing when and why to implement strategies (Pintrich, 2002). Mindfulness—a concept frequently referenced in the discussion on self-care and well-being—is similarly defined as "the practice of being aware of your body, mind, and feelings in the present moment" (Mindfulness, n.d., para. 1). In order to practice metacognition, or mindfulness, Tanner (2012) highlighted the value of educators consistently integrating reflection into learning experiences and assignments.

Motivation. Wolters (1998) advocated recognizing motivation as an equally important component of the learning process, and it is therefore beneficial for consideration in practicing intellectual self-care. Berrett (2012) pointed out that motivation is much more malleable than once believed, "and colleges wield significant power in instilling—and discouraging—it in their students" (para. 2). Students can practice regulating their motivation by blocking out distractions, focusing their attention, improving their physical or emotional readiness to learn, and setting goals for completing tasks (Wolters, 1998).

Growth mindset. Carol Dweck's research and corresponding TED Talks highlight a growth mindset as instrumental toward student learning and success. Dweck (2014) described this mindset as the power of believing you can improve, and Bergland (2017) explained it as a belief that intelligence is malleable—that one can learn from mistakes, especially by practicing self-compassion. Dweck, Walton, and Cohen (2014) argued that challenging students' mindsets about intelligence can make them "more tenacious learners and higher achievers" (p. 17)—which further emphasizes the significance of adopting a growth mindset as a means of caring for the intellectual self. Dweck (2014) also reinforced the importance of teaching students how to move outside their comfort zones in order to learn something new, especially since this process can stimulate the growth of connections between neurons, which enhances brain function.

Resilience and grit. A growth mindset has also been found to "boost resilience, positive emotions, and someone's ability to bounce back quickly from the agony of defeat" (Bergland, 2017, para. 11). Yeager and Dweck (2012) defined resilience as being able to respond to academic or social challenges in ways that are beneficial for development. Duckworth offered a similar concept in her research and TED Talk, defining grit as "perseverance and passion for long-term goals" (Duckworth, 2013; Duckworth, Peterson, Matthews, & Kelly, 2007). Duckworth et al. (2007) added that grit involves working vigorously toward challenges and maintaining both effort and interest despite failures.

Learning dispositions. Because of the recent focus on developing aptitudes and attitudes in students, learning dispositions are of significant value to students as they grow in practicing intellectual self-care. Katz (1988) wrote, "Dispositions . . . can be thought of as habits of mind, tendencies to respond to situations in certain ways" (p. 30). Carr and Claxton (2002) specifically highlighted the dispositions of resilience, playfulness, and reciprocity as central to the pursuit of developing lifelong learners. Learning dispositions, in particular, can be incredibly beneficial for students throughout the learning process because they develop in students a love for the learning process itself—which includes learning to care for themselves.

Educators have two primary responsibilities, both crucial to the learning process: inviting students to understand the purpose of intellectual exercises (Barnett, 2015) and pointing out when students think rightly about their own intellectual engagement. Furthermore, educators ought to model and explain their own metacognitive practices in order to cultivate transfer learning in their students (Pintrich, 2002). With explicit instruction and modeling, educators can help students practice intellectual self-care, resulting in an embodied love of learning, which, in turn, informs how students approach other important forms of self-care.

Caring for the Spiritual Self

Despite the secularization of the academy, studies have revealed an increased interest in religious or spiritual matters among college students (Cherry, Deberg, & Porterfield, 2001; Eck, 2001; Nash, 2001). The Higher Education Research Institute has provided significant longitudinal data regarding the state of students' spirituality. Astin, Astin, Lindholm, and Bryant (2005) concluded students "are searching for deeper meaning . . . looking for ways to cultivate their inner selves, seeking to be compassionate and charitable, and determining what they think and feel about the many issues confronting their society and the global community" (p. 22).

College students across the diverse landscape of higher education are curious about the spiritual dimension of their lives. Students are asking important questions such as:

> Who am I? What are my most deeply felt values? Do I have a
> mission or purpose in my life? Why am I in college? What kind
> of person do I want to become? What sort of world do I want to
> help create? (Astin, Astin, & Lindholm, 2010, p. 1)

Encouraging students to attend to this deeper part of their being—the state of their spirit—matters greatly. Sharon Daloz Parks shared in an interview that educators have an important role in fostering mentoring communities where "big questions are present," helping students access worthy dreams, and inviting them "to imagine a future that can hold significance and purpose both for the self and for the larger world" (Parks & Schwartz, 2007, p. 6). For the purposes of this chapter, the spiritual self will be defined as the inner life of the student. It is the place where students ponder God and the mysteries of life as well as who they are and how they are called to live in the world.

A Theology of Spiritual Self-Care

Smith (2009), while addressing the purpose of Christian higher education, clearly addressed the significance of spiritual self-care. He described education as the "constellation of practices, rituals, and routines that inculcates a particular vision of the good life by inscribing or infusing the vision into the heart (the gut) by means of material, embodied practices" (p. 26). Such practices care for the spirit while simultaneously—and perhaps, ultimately—helping direct students' passions and desires toward the kingdom of God.

Scripture clearly addresses the importance of one's spirit or soul. Matthew 16:26 posed the question, "And what do you benefit if you gain the whole world but lose your own soul? Is anything worth more than your soul?" (NLT). At times, students may find themselves caught up in academic life and the university experience, but what good are those investments if they neglect God and their spirits? Educators must draw awareness to spiritual care, specifically helping students revisit who they are and their life purpose.

Teaching Students to Care for the Spiritual Self

How, then, can educators encourage students to care for their innermost being? For students attending institutions within the United States, in particular, the hustle of university life can crowd out listening to one's own voice as well as God's voice. The following suggestions can serve as starting points for conversations with students and highlight practices to employ with them as they learn to care for their spiritual selves.

Contemplative practices. Astin et al. (2010) found contemplative practices, such as meditation and self-reflection, to be the most impactful tools for enhancing students' spiritual development. Additionally, mind-fulness training, especially within the caring professions—like social work, nursing, and counseling—has been helpful in promoting spiritual aware-ness (Schure, Christopher, & Christopher, 2008; Shapiro, Oman, Thoresen, Plante, & Flinders, 2008; Skovholt & Trotter-Mathison, 2014). The essence of such practices centers on *intention* or "why one is paying attention," *attention* or "moment-to-moment knowing," and *attitude* or "how one pays attention" (Shapiro et al., 2008, p. 2). These practices can take place in a variety of different forms, like journaling, deep breathing, or meditating.

Spiritual disciplines. Within Christian tradition, the history of spiritual disciplines has provided the church with meaningful patterns for seeking God and tending to the spirit. These practices are grounded in Scripture and can serve as a means of grace, or an opportunity for getting under the spout where grace comes out.

It is important to help students realize such activities are not a to-do list but rather rhythms for living in right relationship with God, self, and others (Yankoski, 2014). As such, people often classify spiritual disciplines in accordance with a particular relational intention. Disciplines like sol-itude, silence, fasting, reading Scripture, corporate worship, prayer, or service—both individually and collectively—create space for students in unique ways. Therefore, encouraging students to experiment and explore new disciplines or patterns is important. The spiritual disciplines are meant to provide space to be with God and orient our desires toward his purposes.

Sabbath. One particular discipline worth highlighting is the practice of Sabbath. If students do not know where to start, this spiritual discipline should be considered first. Psalm 46 reminds us to cease striving and, instead, intentionally be still and know God. Sabbath is both a day—an opportunity to intentionally seek rest—and also a disposition to cultivate and practice throughout the week. As Mark Buchanan (2006) described, "A Sabbath heart is restful even in the midst of unrest and upheaval. It is attentive to the presence of God and others even in the welter of much coming and going, rising and falling" (p. 4). It is important for educators to help students realize Sabbath is not merely refraining from working, but it is taking up God's rest.

Caring for the spirit, the innermost part of one's being, is vital in pursuit of human flourishing—especially since the nature of the college experience lends itself toward hustle and busyness. Hindman (2002) recommended inviting students to reflect on and respond to the following questions: "What helps you to feed your deepest hungers? What hinders you? What helps or hinders you from doing or being at your best? What factors help keep you on the path, and which ones can lead you astray?" (p. 169). Educators must utilize questions like these or others to help students listen and respond to their souls—taking a step back to help remember their purposes and nurture their spirits.

Self-Care as a Calling

Of significant value in this process of stepping back is the ability to recall the purpose of self-care itself. The ultimate purpose of self-care, as modeled by Christ, is to grow in capacity to love God and love your neighbor—which is the essence of the Christian vocation. Practicing self-care better equips us to pursue our greatest callings as Christ-followers. Furthermore, when self-care is viewed as a vocational pursuit, it becomes one that is intentionally implemented in *practice*, with *mindfulness* of self and the practice, and one that is *holistic*. This vision also innately helps guard against inclinations toward the frantic pace and narcissism of our individualistic culture. Instead, it grounds self-care as practiced and embodied within the context of community—where many of our ultimate callings lie. Teaching students to care for themselves, therefore, teaches students to more faithfully pursue their callings.

References

American College Health Association. (2017). *American College Health Association-National College Health Assessment II: Undergraduate Student Reference Group Executive Summary Fall 2016.* Hanover, MD: Author.

Ashcraft, P. F., & Gatto, S. L. (2015). Care-of-self in undergraduate nursing students: A pilot study. *Nursing Education Perspectives, 36*(4), 255–256. doi:10.5480/13-1241

Astin, A. W., Astin, H. S., & Lindholm, J. A. (2010). *Cultivating the spirit: How college can enhance students' inner lives.* San Francisco, CA: Jossey-Bass.

Astin, A. W., Astin, H. S., Lindholm, J. A., & Bryant, A. N. (2005). *The spiritual life of college students: A national study of college students' search for meaning and purpose.* Los Angeles, CA: Higher Education Research Institute, UCLA. Retrieved from http://www.spirituality.ucla.edu/docs/reports/Spiritual_Life _College_Students_Full_Report.pdf.

Barnett, M. A. (2015). *Promoting students' intellectual growth.* Retrieved from http://cte.virginia.edu/teaching-tips/promoting-students-intellectual -growth-2/

Benner, D. G. (1984). Emotion. In W. A. Elwell (Ed.), *Evangelical dictionary of theology* (p. 375). Grand Rapids, MI: Baker.

Bergland, C. (2017, January 30). Self-compassion, growth mindset, and the benefits of failure. *Psychology Today.* Retrieved from https://www .psychologytoday.com/blog/the-athletes-way/201701/self-compassion -growth-mindset-and-the-benefits-failure

Berrett, D. (2012, April 15). Can colleges manufacture motivation? *The Chronicle of Higher Education.* Retrieved from http://www.chronicle.com/article /Can-Colleges-Manufacture/131564

Brougham, R. R., Zail, C. M., Mendoza, C. M., & Miller, J. R. (2009). Stress, sex differences, and coping strategies among college students. *Current Psychology, 28,* 85–97. doi:10.1007/s12144-009-9047-0

Brown, B. (2012a). *Daring greatly: How the courage to be vulnerable transforms the way we live, love, parent, and lead.* New York, NY: Avery.

Brown, B. (2012b). *Brené Brown: Listening to shame* [Video file]. Retrieved from https://www.ted.com/talks/brene_brown_listening_to_shame/transcript#t -1219033

Buchanan, M. (2006). *The rest of God: Restoring your soul by restoring Sabbath.* Nashville, TN: Thomas Nelson.

Buckworth, J., & Nigg, C. (2004). Physical activity, exercise, and sedentary behavior in college students. *Journal of American College Health, 53,* 28–34. doi:10.3200/JACH.53.1.28-34

Butler, S. M., Black, D. R., Blue, C. L., & Gretebeck, R. J. (2004). Change in diet, physical activity, and body weight in female college freshman. *American Journal of Health Behavior, 28,* 24–32. Retrieved from https://pdfs .semanticscholar.org/df12/fe460c099ec56e26c7eac3215b683fbbb2cd.pdf

Capanna, C., Stratta, P., Collazzoni, A., D'Ubaldo, V., Pacifico, R., Di Emidio, G., . . . Rossi, A. (2013). Social connectedness as resource of resilience: Italian validation of the Social Connectedness Scale-Revised. *Journal of Psychopathology, 19,* 320–326. Retrieved from http://www.jpsychopathol.it /wp-content/uploads/2015/07/SOPSI-4-13.pdf

Carr, M., & Claxton, G. (2002). Tracking the development of learning dispositions. *Assessment in Education: Principles, Policy, and Practice, 9,* 9–37. doi:10.1080/09695940220119148

Cherry, C., Deberg, B. A., & Porterfield, A. (2001). *Religion on campus: What religion really means to today's undergraduates.* Chapel Hill, NC: University of North Carolina Press.

Crombie, A. P., Ilich, J. Z., Dutton, G. R., Panton, L. B., & Abood, D. A. (2009). The freshman weight gain phenomenon revisited. *Nutrition Reviews, 67,* 83–94. doi:10.1111/j.1753-4887.2008.00143.x

Damasio, A. (1994). *Descartes' error: Emotion, reason, and the human brain.* New York, NY: Grosset/Putnam.

DePaul University Teaching Commons. (2017). *Activities for metacognition.* Retrieved from https://resources.depaul.edu/teaching-commons /teaching-guides/learning-activities/Pages/activities-for-metacognition.aspx

Duckworth, A. (2013, April). *Grit: The power of passion and perseverance* [Video file]. Retrieved from https://www.ted.com/talks/angela_lee_duckworth_grit _the_power_of_passion_and_perseverance#t-356937

Duckworth, A. L., Peterson, C., Matthews, M. D., & Kelly, D. R. (2007). Grit: Perseverance and passion for long-term goals. *Journal of Personality and Social Psychology, 92,* 1087–1101. doi:10.1037/0022-3514.92.6.1087

Dweck, C. (2014, November). *The power of believing that you can improve* [Video file]. Retrieved from https://www.ted.com/talks/carol_dweck _the_power_of_believing_that_you_can_improve

Dweck, C. S., Walton, G. M., & Cohen, G. L. (2014). *Academic tenacity: Mindsets and skills that promote long-term learning.* Retrieved from http:// k12education.gatesfoundation.org/download/?Num=2807&filename=30 -Academic-Tenacity.pdf

Dwyer, A. L., & Cummings, A. L. (2001). Stress, self-efficacy, social support, and coping strategies in university students. *Canadian Journal of Counseling, 35,* 208–220. Retrieved from http://cjc-rcc.ucalgary.ca/cjc/index.php/rcc/article /view/189/430

Dyson, R., & Renk, K. (2006). Freshmen adaptation to university life: Depressive symptoms, stress, and coping. *Journal of Clinical Psychology, 62,* 1231–1244. doi:10.1002/jclp.20295

Eck, D. L. (2001). *A new religious America: How a "Christian country" has now become the world's most religiously diverse nation.* San Francisco, CA: Harper San Francisco.

Edwards, J. (1821). *A treatise concerning religious affections: In three parts.* Philadelphia, PA: James Crissy.

English, L. (2009). *College students' perceived benefits, barriers, and cues to vigorous physical activity* (Master's thesis). Retrieved from OhioLINK. (ucin1258663443)

Extremera, N., & Fernández-Berrocal, P. (2006). Emotional intelligence as predictor of mental, social, and physical health in university students. *The Spanish Journal of Psychology, 9,* 45–51. doi:10.1017/S1138741600005965

Ferrara, C. M. (2009). The college experience: Physical activity, nutrition, and implications for intervention and future research. *Journal of Exercise Physiology Online, 12*(1), 23–35. Retrieved from https://www.asep.org/asep/asep/Ferrara12_1_23-35.pdf

Gates, J. (2015). Self-care: A Christian perspective. *Evangelical Review of Theology, 39*(1), 4–17. Retrieved from http://bit.ly/2DGUA9X

Halpern, D. F. (1999). Teaching for critical thinking: Helping college students develop the skills and dispositions of a critical thinker. *New Directions for Teaching and Learning, 80,* 69–74. doi:10.1002/tl.8005

Hindman, D. M. (2002). From splintered lives to whole persons: Facilitating spiritual development in college students. *Religious Education, 97,* 165–182. doi:10.1080/00344080290060923

Huang, T. T. K., Harris, K. J., Lee, R. E., Nazir, N., Born, W., & Kaur, H. (2003). Assessing overweight, obesity, diet, and physical activity in college students. *Journal of American College Health, 52,* 83–86. doi:10.1080/07448480309595728

Jeffries, C., Spagna, M., & Behring, S. T. (2017, August 18). Toward a culture of self-care. *Inside Higher Ed.* Retrieved from https://www.insidehighered.com/views/2017/08/18/value-self-care-programs-campuses-essay

Jennings, W. (2015, October 30). Willie Jennings: To be a Christian intellectual. *Yale Divinity School.* Retrieved from http://divinity.yale.edu/news/willie-jennings-be-christian-intellectual

Katz, A., Davis, P., & Findlay, S. S. (2002). Ask and ye shall plan: A health needs assessment of a university population. *Canadian Journal of Public Health, 93,* 63–66. Retrieved from http://www.jstor.org/stable/41993696

Katz, L. G. (1988). What should young children be doing? *American Educator, 12*(2), 29–45.

Keating, X. D., Guan, J., Piñero, J. C., & Bridges, D. M. (2005). A meta-analysis of college students' physical activity behaviors. *Journal of American College Health, 54*, 116–126. doi:10.3200/JACH.54.2.116-126

Kraut, R., Patterson, M., Lundmark, V., Kiesler, S., Mukopadhvav, T., & Scherlis, W. (1998). Internet paradox: A social technology that reduces social involvement and psychological well-being? *American Psychologist, 53*, 1017–1031. doi:10.1037/0003-066X.53.9.1017

Kuhn, D., & Dean, D., Jr. (2004). Metacognition: A bridge between cognitive psychology and educational practice. *Theory Into Practice, 43*, 268–273. doi:10.1207/s15430421tip4304_4

Landau, M. J., Oyserman, D., Keefer, L. A., & Smith, G. C. (2014). The college journey and academic engagement: How metaphor use enhances identity-based motivation. *Journal of Personality and Social Psychology, 106*, 679–698. doi:10.1037/a0036414

Mindfulness. (n.d.). In *Cambridge Advanced Learner's Dictionary and Thesaurus.* Retrieved from https://dictionary.cambridge.org/us/dictionary/english/mindfulness

Moses, J., Bradley, G. L., & O'Callaghan, F. V. (2016). When college students look after themselves: Self-care practices and well-being. *Journal of Student Affairs Research and Practice, 53*, 346–359. doi:10.1080/19496591.2016.1157488

Nash, R. J. (2001). *Religious pluralism in the academy: Opening the dialogue.* New York, NY: Peter Lang.

National Wellness Institute. (1976). *Six dimensions of wellness model.* Retrieved from http://c.ymcdn.com/sites/www.nationalwellness.org/resource/resmgr/docs/sixdimensionsfactsheet.pdf

Nelson, M. C., Lust, K., Story, M., & Ehlinger, E. (2008). Credit card debt, stress and key health risk behaviors among college students. *American Journal of Health Promotion, 22*, 400–406. doi:10.4278/ajhp.22.6.400

Nouwen, H. (1995, Spring). From solitude to community to ministry. *Christianity Today Leadership Journal.* Retrieved from http://www.christianitytoday.com/pastors/1995/spring/5l280.html

Parks, S. D., & Schwartz, L. M. (2007, November). The undergraduate quest for meaning, purpose, and faith: An interview with Sharon Daloz Parks. *Spirituality in Higher Education Newsletter, 4*(1). Retrieved from http://spirituality.ucla.edu/docs/newsletters/4/Parks_Final.pdf

Pauline, J. (2013). Physical activity behaviors, motivation, and self-efficacy among college students. *College Student Journal, 47*(1), 64–74.

Pintrich, P. R. (2002). The role of metacognitive knowledge in learning, teaching, and assessing. *Theory Into Practice, 41,* 219–225. doi:10.1207/ s15430421tip4104_3

Reetz, D. R., Bershad, C., LeViness, P., & Whitlock, M. (2016). *The association for university and college counseling center directors annual survey.* Retrieved from https://taucccd.memberclicks.net/assets/documents /aucccd%202016%20monograph%20-%20public.pdf

Rusche, S. N., & Jason, K. (2011). "You have to absorb yourself in it": Using inquiry and reflection to promote student learning and self-knowledge. *Teaching Sociology, 39,* 338–353. doi:10.1177/0092055X11418685

Salovey, P., & Grewal, D. (2005). The science of emotional intelligence. *Current Directions in Psychological Science, 14,* 281–285. doi:10.1111 /j.0963-7214.2005.00381.x

Salovey, P., & Mayer, J. D. (1990). Emotional intelligence. *Imagination, Cognition and Personality, 9,* 185–211. doi:10.2190/DUGG-P24E-52WK-6CDG

Sasaki, M., & Yamasaki, K. (2007). Stress coping and the adjustment process among university freshmen. *Counselling Psychology Quarterly, 20,* 51–67. doi:10.1080/09515070701219943

Schure, M. B., Christopher, J., & Christopher, S. (2008). Mind–body medicine and the art of self-care: Teaching mindfulness to counseling students through yoga, meditation, and qigong. *Journal of Counseling & Development, 86,* 47–56. doi:10.1002/j.1556-6678.2008.tb00625.x

Shapiro, S. L., Oman, D., Thoresen, C. E., Plante, T. G., & Flinders, T. (2008). Cultivating mindfulness: Effects on well-being. *Journal of Clinical Psychology, 64,* 840–862. doi:10.1002/jclp.20491

Skovholt, T. M., & Trotter-Mathison, M. (2014). *The resilient practitioner: Burnout prevention and self-care strategies for counselors, therapists, teachers, and health professionals.* New York, NY: Routledge.

Small, M., Bailey-Davis, L., Morgan, N., & Maggs, J. (2013). Changes in eating and physical activity behaviors across seven semesters of college: Living on or off campus matters. *Health Education & Behavior, 40,* 435–441. doi:10.1177/1090198112467801

Smith, J. K. A. (2009). *Desiring the kingdom: Worship, worldview, and cultural formation.* Grand Rapids, MI: Baker Academic.

Soderstrom, M., Dolbier, C., Leiferman, J., & Steinhardt, M. (2000). The relationship of hardiness, coping strategies, and perceived stress to symptoms of illness. *Journal of Behavioral Medicine, 23,* 311–328. doi:10.1023/A:3A1005514310142

Sparling, P. B., & Snow, T. K. (2002). Physical activity patterns in recent college alumni. *Research Quarterly for Exercise and Sport, 73*, 200–205. doi:10.1080/0 2701367.2002.10609009

Sperling, R. A., Howard, B. C., Staley, R., & DuBois, N. (2004). Metacognition and self-regulated learning constructs. *Educational Research and Evaluation, 10*, 117–139. doi:10.0.4.52/edre.10.2.117.27905

Stark, M. A., Hoekstra, T., Hazel, D. L., & Barton, B. (2012). Caring for self and others: Increasing health care students' healthy behaviors. *Work: Journal of Prevention, Assessment & Rehabilitation, 42*, 393–401. doi:10.3233/WOR -2012-1428

Stott, J. R. W. (1984, April 20). Am I supposed to love myself or hate myself? *Christianity Today*, 26–28.

Tanner, K. D. (2012). Promoting student metacognition. *CBE—Life Science Education, 11*, 113–120. doi:10.1187/cbe.12-03-0033

Twenge, J. M. (2017, September). Have smartphones destroyed a generation? *The Atlantic*. Retrieved from https://www.theatlantic.com/magazine/archive /2017/09/has-the-smartphone-destroyed-a-generation/534198/

U.S. National Center for Health Statistics (2012). *Healthy People 2010 Final Review*. Washington, DC: U.S. Government Printing Office.

Wolters, C. A. (1998). Self-regulated learning and college students' regulation of motivation. *Journal of Educational Psychology, 90*(2), 224–235.

Wolterstorff, N. (2004). *Educating for shalom: Essays on Christian higher education*. Grand Rapids, MI: Eerdmans.

Yankoski, M. (2014). *The sacred year: Mapping the soulscape of spiritual practice— how contemplating apples, living in a cave and befriending a dying woman revived my life*. Nashville, TN: W Publishing.

Yeager, D. S., & Dweck, C. S. (2012). Mindsets that promote resilience: When students believe that personal characteristics can be developed. *Educational Psychologist, 47*, 302–314. doi:10.1080/00461520.2012.722805

Zeidner, M., Matthews, G., & Roberts, R. D. (2009). *What we know about emotional intelligence: How it affects learning, work, relationships, and our mental health*. Cambridge, MA: MIT Press.

5

A CALL FOR HOLISTIC INTELLECTUAL CARE OF UNIVERSITY STUDENTS

An Essay for the Twenty-First-Century Academy

ANITA FITZGERALD HENCK

Azusa Pacific University

On thousands of residential campuses across the United States, new student orientations launch on a warm summer day in late August and represent the culmination of several years of family college visits and many months of campus-wide planning for freshman move-in. Whether the campus is a liberal arts college in Smalltown, USA, or a large state university in the midst of a major metropolitan area, some characteristics are the same. The day is filled with eager students, anxious parents, watchful campus safety officials, and highly motivated student leaders greeting vehicles overfilled with people and possessions. Energy levels are high, fatigue is real, and anticipation is a bittersweet emotion.

Parents are proud of their students' university acceptances while also preoccupied with family finances and campus safety. Students are excited about newfound independence, yet nervous about making friends as they meet fellow first-year students in a sea of new faces. Senior administrators muster the energy to exhibit excitement, even if it is their second or third decade of fall opening events. Student leaders eagerly live into the enthusiasm of their newly elected roles, delighted to be upperclass students tasked with welcoming the latest group of newcomers. Resident directors, student activities staff, and other student development personnel have just concluded weeks of student leader training and last-minute housing adjustments for late depositors, while juggling personal guilt about long workweeks where they have been away from their own families and homes. And faculty are busy making final syllabi changes, while preparing for last-minute schedule adjustments and new teaching assignments caused by under-enrolled course cancellations. All the while, they distractedly attend well-intentioned faculty development sessions on mapping student learning outcomes to each course's defined objectives (in preparation for an accreditation visit four years in the future).

Busy, hurried, invested, excited, nervous—these are the adjectives that pervade descriptions used by students, parents, administrators, and student leaders to describe the start of a new academic year on residential campuses across the United States. Yet, despite their fatigue, all campus members will gather the needed energy to provide heartfelt greetings to eager eighteen-year-olds and their families. On some campuses, cabinet and board members will breathe a sigh of relief and offer up a private prayer of thanksgiving that campus enrollments are sufficiently strong to wholeheartedly celebrate as they begin another school year. And, on a few campuses, the news will be considerably less robust. Worries will begin for the financial reality of the new year with enrollments substantially below projections and likely reductions in budgets and staffing. With few variations, this cycle is repeated year after year, campus after campus, at thousands of institutions across the United States.

Yet, while these core cocurricular activities are embedded into the life cycle of our campuses, the principal purpose of college-going—the intellectual care and development of our students—has gradually morphed over time. This focus has shifted from being defined by the cultivation and stewardship of the life of the mind to a primary focus on the academy's development of unique and well-defined academic programs that aid in this process. Consequently, intellectual development is often defined as an end product of academic programs and degrees rather than by the collaborative process for advancing the holistic intellectual growth and development of students. This market-driven focus on the end product of higher education—instead of emphasizing the importance of the means by which we help students advance intellectually—has, in some cases, minimized our shared responsibilities as educators for the intellectual care of our students.

The relationship between explicit (or concrete) knowledge and tacit knowledge—the ineffable by-products of intellectual development—is at the heart of holistic intellectual care. Notably, the de facto emphasis on explicit knowledge that can readily be transmitted from instructor to student, textbook to reader, or academic program to degree-earning student has become the product for which the academy is known and by which it often defines itself. The holistic intellectual care of university students emphasizes both the means of the academy's transmittal and cultivation of knowledge, as well as the stewardship of the life of the mind. When the means become our end, we are impoverished. Many institutions and academic programs expand their investment beyond explicit knowledge transmittal to include the impact of tacit knowledge. But the reality is that, far too often, more emphasis is placed on academic content than on the holistic intellectual care and development of our students.

In twenty-first-century American higher education, our focused language of retention, academic success, time-to-completion, graduate school admissions, and employability has become the measurable outcome of the academic work of our institutions. The resulting impact is significant, both for our students and society at large. Whereas recent decades have seen campuses focus on intentional cultivation of their students' holistic cocurricular development, there has been less focus on the holistic intellectual care of students. Without an intentional focus on intellectual care, we risk becoming primarily performance- or measurement-driven in our assertions about the quality of our academic progress, and in doing so, we can lose critical opportunities for the creative development of the human mind. While this reality does not mean that academic programs or human minds are no longer creative nor cultivated, it does mean the academy is less intentional about planning for and ensuring the intellectual care of our students than it is invested in the planning of student recruitment and orientation activities. Consequently, the measure of our intellectual cultivation is now the array of academic programs and services offered.

Now more than ever, it seems important that we temporarily put aside institutional reviews that focus on managerial routines and cyclical tasks of university life. Instead, it is time to ask what we could accomplish if we invested similar time, resources, and commitment to our twenty-first-century vision of the role and impact of the academy on intellectual growth and development of our students.

The guiding question is this—"How do we provide for the intellectual care of our students?"—with the corollary probe of "How did we move away from the centrality of this important task?" Before we measure where we are in contrast with where we want to be, it seems important to take a retrospective look at how we began focusing on programs as a measure of our engagement in intellectual development and care.

Historical Context of Universities

While the origins of postsecondary education are rooted in North Africa and the Middle East in the late first and early second century AD and in Europe in the early 1000s, U.S. higher education began at Harvard College in 1636, even before the founding of this new country. Today, Harvard exemplifies a pantheon of the changes that our profession has experienced, including a change from its early motto of *Veritas Christo et Ecclesiae* or "Truth for Christ and the Church" to the current version—*Veritas* or "Truth" (Morison, 1998, p. 43). Some would question if the present-day quest for truth for the sake of truth has contributed to the loss of our historical pursuit of truth for a purpose greater than ourselves.

Since the early development of colleges in the United States, these institutions were places for deep learning of the classics and places that intentionally fostered the accomplishment of key developmental tasks—both intellectual and psychosocial—of emerging young adults. Yet, as exemplified in the documentary film *Ivory Tower* (Rossi, 2014), contemporary student and parent campus visits and selection processes typically focus on comparing information about four-year student degree completion rates and job prospects versus classic indicators such as the educational pedigree and scholarly accomplishments of the faculty, as well as institutional renown. However, this change is not just a recent phenomenon.

According to a 2015 article in *The Chronicle of Higher Education* entitled "The Day the Purpose of College Changed," the redirection of collegiate purpose began fifty years ago. On February 28, 1967, when faced with a significant state budget crisis in California, then-Governor Ronald Reagan gave a speech in which he promised to do no harm to the state's three-tiered public system of higher education. Yet his follow-up remark was, "We do believe that there are certain intellectual luxuries that perhaps we could do without for a little while at least" (as cited in Berrett, 2015, para. 3).

While it might be simplistic to find a singular date on which our primary purpose changed, the concept of "intellectual luxury" being sacrificed for a focus on education for purposeful employment continues as a significant tension a half century after Reagan's seminal declaration. And, while it is entirely possible to meet competing priorities—broad education for the public good, as well as employability for the nation's and individual's economic good—it is also important that the significant responsibility for the intellectual good be purposefully addressed within the academy. The case could be made that focus on the importance of intellectual care has been subordinated to conversations of academic success and both curricular and cocurricular outcomes. These subtexts have become the primary, guiding concepts for American academic administrators of the twenty-first century.

Historical Context of Student Care

More than eighty years ago, the American Council on Education convened a conversation among educators whose focus on student engagement extended beyond the walls of the classroom. The resulting 1937 document, *The Student Personnel Point of View*, and its revised 1949 version served as the founding documents for the launch of a new profession—college student affairs (NASPA, n.d.).

This profession has grown over time to include core student services such as residential life, food service, athletics, counseling, career services, student activities, multicultural affairs, and spiritual development, with sectors such as orientation, advising, campus safety, community service, writing support, learning enrichment centers, and others housed in various divisions within institutional organizational charts. Nonetheless, the formal recognition of cocurricular student services enjoys over eighty years of history and a remarkable investment in campus culture and practices.

Meanwhile, Arthur Chickering's formative work *Education and Identity* was published in 1969 and included findings from a decade-long project with which he had been involved: "The Project on Student Development in Small Colleges." Among this work's notable contributions to the field of college student affairs was the identification of seven developmental tasks of traditional-aged college students that Chickering titled "vectors." Chickering's college student identity theory, in concert with the emerging prominence of Student Affairs Administrators in Higher Education (NASPA—formerly known as the National Association of Student Personnel Administrators), influenced generations of conversations and inspired the emergence of cocurricular programs and student personnel services on U.S. college and university campuses.

Present-Day Focus

Increased postsecondary education and the growth of cocurricular programs and services have supported increased numbers of college-going students. The corollary emphasis on academic programs drew the field of higher education away from a traditional focus on intellectual development through a series of moves that resulted in a proliferation of new institutions of higher education with specialized career preparation foci. This changing emphasis is not a new phenomenon, as it began in the days of teacher colleges and agricultural schools and moved to the present array of specialized schools within universities that focus on niche professional preparation.

While addressing important societal needs by preparing a workforce, these changes led to a loss of intentional intellectual care, which has profound implications, both individually and societally.

Ironically, it seems that today's most urgent higher education conversations no longer need to focus on the cocurricular care of college students, as those aspects are typically well-articulated, planned, and practiced on most campuses. Instead, our conversations about holistic student care must devote more time to the intellectual care of college students. This discourse is needed to ensure that the central purpose for collegiate education of providing a broad liberal arts education, cultivating critical thinking skills, and developing global citizens is given necessary attention. And this discourse will cause us to refocus our efforts regarding the intellectual care of college students.

Parks and Bloom: Two Perspectives

Sharon Daloz Parks's *Big Questions, Worthy Dreams* (2000) examined the breadth of developmental venues of the traditional collegiate years and urged adult engagement in the formative mentoring of both young adults and their culture. In defining higher education as one of a number of mentoring communities with which individuals in their late teens and early twenties interact, Parks also identified other venues as being the professions, the workplace, travel, the natural environment, families, and religious faith communities. Yet, she specifically identified the collegiate community as a place for mentoring and cultivating "imagination" (p. 158). The conundrum of epistemological assumptions of the academy about its students is described in this way:

> The academy tends to perceive students either as independent
> thinkers prepared to make objective judgments about compet-
> ing alternatives or as conventional, dependent neophytes in
> need of being awakened to the complex and relative character
> of all knowledge. These assumptions and this ambivalence have
> extended to residence hall and extracurricular life, where *in loco*

parentis once prevailed but where, on the one hand, students are now regarded as adult (read: rational) and, on the other hand, presumed to be in a process of cognitive-affective-social-moral development. If, however, these aspects of development are recognized . . . they [are not] regarded as central to the purposes of the college or university. (p. 160)

Parks further noted,

The domain of knowledge has been reduced to the domain of objective reality (understood as empirical fact and theoretical analysis abstracted from fact, standing in contrast to ultimate reality). . . . Reason and knowledge, thus defined, are reduced to those processes that can be analyzed and replicated—in short, produced and controlled. (p. 160)

While the academy exists with boundaries on the relativity of truth, the potential engagement of the whole person in discourse provides unique opportunities for expanding "big questions of purpose, personal meaning, and social concern" (Parks, 2000, p. 163). The need and responsibility for broader engagement of faculty and students alike provides opportunity for developing the life of the mind in concert with the life of faith, emotion, person, society, and culture. For this development to occur, we must first develop an updated view of the present-day academy and refocus our meaning and purpose for existence. Ironically, this process may return us full circle to the education of the whole person, moving beyond the cocurricular preparation of individuals who are in pursuit of a collegiate degree.

Moving from a historical focus solely on the cultivation of the intellectual being to an emphasis on holistic student development had unintended consequences. Notably, the development of the life of the mind has been redefined to primarily include more concrete aspects of academic programs. But it is rarely defined in terms of nurturing and cultivating creative or innovative ideas. We laud creativity in market-successful projects and products but rarely in intellectual concepts in and of themselves. And it is infrequent that the university's role in intellectual care is defined in terms of the stewardship of unique characteristics of each human's psycho-cognitive potential.

In Allan Bloom's (1987) bestseller *The Closing of the American Mind: How Higher Education Has Failed Democracy and Impoverished the Souls of Today's Students,* his early premise is that "the liberally educated person is one who is able to resist the easy and preferred answers, not because he is obstinate but because he knows others worthy of consideration" (Bloom, 1987/2012, p. 21). His analysis of the role of the university in developing minds skilled for the intellectual tasks of a liberal arts education finds it lacking, with some disciplines present "because they wandered in recently to perform some job demanded of the university" (p. 337). By contrast, "liberal education should give the student the sense that learning must and can be both synoptic and precise" (p. 343). He faulted the university as being complicit in this critique:

> [The] crisis of liberal education is a reflection of a crisis at the peaks of learning, an incoherence and incompatibility among the first principles with which we interpret the world, an intel-lectual crisis of the greatest magnitude, which constitutes the crisis of our civilization. But perhaps it would be true to say that the crisis consists not so much in this incoherence but in our incapacity to discuss or even recognize it. Liberal education flourished when it prepared the way for the discussion of a uni-fied view of nature and man's place in it, which the best minds debated on the highest level. It decayed when what lay beyond it were only specialties, the premises of which do not lead to any such vision. (pp. 346–347)

The Heart of Higher Education

The growing concern about the commodification of higher education is rooted in observations that academic program structures and measur-able outcomes masquerade as intellectual development of students. The consequent mourning by purists who are committed to intellectual pursuits focuses on the lack of time and space for the creativity of collaboration, the insights borne of time for reflection, and the intellectual sharpening that occurs through critique, disagreement, and new ways of understanding. In *The Heart of Higher Education,* Palmer and Zajonc (2010) observed,

> The academy has largely lost one of its most critical preconditions: the quietude that allows for real reflection on what we have seen and heard, felt, and thought, a quietude that has been overwhelmed by overactivity and frenzy of the same sort found in many workplaces. . . . [O]ne of the academy's taproots is the monastery, a bastion of quietude established in the fourth century . . . [A]s the scope of schooling expanded, the quietude declined and disappeared. Our lives are so frenetic, and our models of inquiry so argumentative, aggressive, and even combative, that we do not even know what we have lost. (p. 145)

The distress reflected by Bloom (1987/2012), as well as Palmer and Zajonc (2010), is more than an elitist protectionism of a classic strand of both pedagogy and content within higher education. It is a deeper concern for the impact of the loss of intellectual cultivation of individuals, communities, and society at large. As educators, it is important that we take stock of the gradual reorientation—decision by decision, academic year by academic year, and era by era—of the academy's move away from the creativity that results from space to innovate, from robust intellectual debate, and from interdisciplinary discourse with a goal of improving our understanding of the common good.

Due to our impoverished attention to the intellectual care of both students and scholars, we have lost emphasis on the cultivation of the mind, while focusing on credentialing the individual. Our present call is to the intellectual care of all members of the academy, to foster open dialogue without a formal agenda, and to make a commitment to an epistemological reflective process that advances the life of the mind.

A Reprise for Higher Education

With deep investment in the student collegiate experience, higher education has provided important programs and services that enhance the holistic psychosocial development of students. Yet, in so doing, in many settings, we have focused on self-examination through spirituality, mindfulness, and other opportunities while developing less creative venues for academic exploration. Some might say we have lost our focus and strayed from the primary goal of college—developing and cultivating an academic arena that fosters intellectual development and care.

In 2016, the Association of American Colleges and Universities (AAC&U) reported on the conversations of a gathering of presidents who discussed reclaiming higher education as a public good. They noted the need for models of civil discourse, civic engagement, and the betterment of society as an important goal and as attainable if we engage competing priorities—liberal education for the sake of learning and employability for the betterment of society. While acknowledging the important and contemporary focus on education for employability, the AAC&U presidents' conversation led to this commitment: "Together, we can liberate mindsets by focusing not on the strictly defined goal of employment, but on the more humane and capacious goals of a better life, better communities, and a better society" (Sutton, 2016, para. 4).

The question of whether it is possible to return to our intellectual roots as our primary focus is both real and sobering. Present-day higher education is designed on a model of inputs and outputs, which has become big business. And some fear that design leaves little margin for broad cultivation of an ineffable goal such as intellectual care. Bloom (1987/2012) concluded his treatise on higher education's failings by writing,

> These are the shadows cast by the peaks of the university over the entering undergraduate. Together they represent what the university has to say about man and his education, and they do not project a coherent image. The differences and the indifferences are too great. It is difficult to imagine that there is either

the wherewithal or the energy within the university to constitute
or reconstitute the idea of an educated human being and establish a liberal education again. (p. 380)

Perhaps we have moved too far into the business-model design and policy
complexities of higher education, resulting in its structured academic programs, for us to reconstitute an idyllic concept where education is discovery-
based contemplative learning. However, perhaps all is not lost in the tension
between education for a career purpose and education as a means to discover and cultivate the potential of the mind. In calling higher education
into a place of integrative learning, Palmer and Zajonc (2010) wrote,

> We are being called into a more paradoxical wholeness of know-
> ing by many voices. There is a new commitment of scholars in
> a variety of fields now who understand that genuine knowing
> comes out of a healthy dance between the objective and the
> subjective, between the analytic and the integrative, between the
> experimental and what I would call the receptive. So, I am not
> trying to split these paradoxes apart; I am trying to put them
> back together. (p. x)

Our challenge and opportunity as educators is to create an expectation that
the collegiate experience will ensure intellectual development and provide
intellectual care. This shift might include providing sectors of unregulated
time for our students to wrestle with big ideas and questions, creating
venues for broadly participatory intellectual discourse, and engaging more
intentionally and fully the life of the mind beyond the classroom. At mini-
mum, it is a recognition that explicit knowledge transmittal is transactional
while tacit knowledge development is transformational. As Palmer and
Zajonc (2010) acknowledged, it will take a healthy dance to reimagine the
logistics of delivering academic programs and providing creative time and
space for holistic integrated learning. But it will provide both opportunity
and expectation for Parks's big questions and worthy dreams.

Postlude

As someone who has invested my entire professional life in higher education (with roles as staff assistant to the provost, vice president for student
life, professor, and now dean of education), the persistent tension between
the life of the mind and the life of the academy has long been a personal
fascination and concern. With deep respect for the needs and benefits of
accreditation, assessment, policies, and procedures, I also have arrived at
a clear understanding that working solely to institutional task instead of
developing leadership vision can limit creativity and thwart breakthroughs
if rigidly followed.

Despite my inclination for an "ordered life," there have been many situations where time-bound structures have required a project to conclude
before it was truly complete. Though administrative deadlines might have
been satisfied, the disappointment of "what could have been" often remains
when projects conclude by timetable but are less developed and impactful
than they might have been. The call is to model that, as lifelong learners
and educators, we are more valuable than the degrees we award or earn.
The very process of learning is transformative but not formulaic. And, in
cultivating the love of learning beyond the walls of the academy and for a
lifetime, we do our best work.

As young newlyweds, my husband and I bought a piece of calligraphy
art by Michael Podesta (1979) that has held a visible place in each of our
five homes over the last four decades. It serves as a fitting reminder for
those of us committed to the holistic development of ourselves. And, as
academics, it calls us to create ways to cultivate intellectual development
and care for our students (and ourselves). It reads,

> If, as Herod, we fill our lives with things, and again with things,
> If we consider ourselves so unimportant that we must fill every
>   moment of our lives with action,
> When will we have time to make the long, slow journey across
>   the desert as did the Magi?

Or sit and watch the stars as did the Shepherds?
Or brood over the coming of the child as did Mary?
For each one of us there is a desert to travel, a star to discover,
    and a being within ourselves to bring to life.[1] (Podesta, 1979)

---

[1] The original author of the text for this artwork is widely unknown, but it was likely abbreviated from the December 1920 issue of *The Association Monthly* published by the Young Women's Christian Association of the U.S.A. and circulated without attribution.

References

Berrett, D. (2015, January 25). The day the purpose of college changed. *The Chronicle of Higher Education*. Retrieved from http://www.chronicle.com /article/The-Day-the-Purpose-of-College/151359/

Bloom, A. (2012). *The closing of the American mind: How higher education has failed democracy and impoverished the souls of today's students* (Rev. ed.). New York, NY: Simon & Schuster Paperbacks. (Original work published 1987)

Chickering, A. (1969). *Education and identity*. San Francisco, CA: Jossey-Bass.

Morison, S. E. (1998). *The founding of Harvard College*. Cambridge, MA: Harvard University Press.

NASPA. (n.d.). About student affairs. Retrieved from https://www.naspa.org /about/student-affairs

Palmer, P. J., & Zajonc, A. (2010). *The heart of higher education: A call to renewal*. San Francisco, CA: Jossey-Bass.

Parks, S. J. (2000). *Big questions, worthy dreams: Mentoring young adults in their search for meaning, purpose, and faith*. San Francisco, CA: Jossey-Bass.

Podesta, M. (1979). *Desert* [Unpublished art]. Retrieved from http://www .michaelpodesta.com/Desert-p53.html

Rossi, A. (Writer, Director, & Producer). (2014). *Ivory Tower* [Motion Picture]. United States: Participant Media, Paramount Pictures, and Samuel Goldwyn Films.

Sutton, B. Z. (2016, June 20). Higher education's public purpose. *LEAP*. Retrieved from https://www.aacu.org/leap/liberal-education-nation-blog /higher-educations-public-purpose

6

SOLIDARITY AND MUTUALITY AS AN ETHIC OF CARE *WITH* STUDENTS OF COLOR

TABATHA L. JONES JOLIVET

Azusa Pacific University

KAREN A. LONGMAN

Azusa Pacific University

Early Christian writers claimed that transcending social and ethnic differences by sharing meals, homes, and worship with persons of different backgrounds was a proof of the truth of the Christian faith
(Pohl, 1999, p. 5).

In this chapter, we consider how solidarity and mutuality can serve as a prism through which to imagine an ethic of caring *with* students of color in Christian higher education. As colleagues co-laboring to write this chapter, we intentionally make visible the distinctiveness of our own lenses, voices, identities, and lived experiences to exemplify what it means to embody both solidarity and mutuality. We also build upon the work of our colleagues, Collins and Jun (2017), who examined the white architecture of the mind. In doing so, we employ design metaphors to ground an ethic of caring in a theology that calls for mutuality and solidarity in *structure* and *practice*.

"An Open Door That No One Can Shut"

The imagery of doors may seem like an odd way to introduce a chapter that addresses how Christians in higher education—and individuals working in Christian colleges and universities more specifically—can embody an ethic of care with students of color. All of us can think back on certain doors that seemed to have been firmly closed to us. In some cases, that closed door elicited a sign of relief for the clarity offered when a decision needed to be made. Equally formative on the journey of life are doors that have spontaneously seemed to open wide, beckoning us to take a new path into different or wider opportunities. In this chapter, we consider the imagery of doors, and later walls, to discuss how and why Christian higher education can and should model a commitment to diversity, equity, and inclusion in applying an ethic of care in our campus contexts.

I (Karen) believe that the doors referenced in the opening chapters of the book of Revelation can be instructive in regard to the attitudes and behaviors that Christ desires of us as believers and adherents to kingdom values. At a personal level and by way of introduction, when I think of the doors (open or closed) that have been influential in my own life, I am thankful to have begun my career by spending nearly twenty years based in Washington, DC, learning the landscape of Christian higher education and visiting over eighty campuses in my role as vice president for professional development and research with the Council for Christian Colleges & Universities (CCCU). During those years, I worked with amazing people who served on the Racial Harmony Council, cheered as two full-time staff were hired to create the Office of Racial/Ethnic Diversity, attended conferences that offered programming and networking for the people of color on CCCU campuses, and subsequently have had the privilege of partnering with teams of resource leaders to offer a series of multi-ethnic leadership development institutes (M-E LDIs) since 2011. It was at the June 2015 M-E LDI that the vision for a book project took shape, with twenty authors coming together in June 2016 to draft initial versions of the chapters now available in *Diversity Matters: Race, Ethnicity, and the Future of Higher Education* (Longman, 2017).

Having the initial door of working at the CCCU open, walking through other doors that contributed to deep friendships with M-E LDI participants and others, and occasionally pushing on doors where I felt burdened to support change—all of these have enriched my life and hopefully contributed constructively to the purpose of this chapter. Yet as Tabatha and I have tackled this topic together, I defer to the lessons she has learned through many years of experience as a student affairs professional at Pepperdine University and the "deep dive" of her dissertation research under Daryl Smith at Claremont Graduate School. Additionally, I honor the ways in which she loves and cares for all students in Azusa Pacific University's doctoral programs (EdD and PhD), knowing that she personifies the best of what we hope for ourselves in caring for (and with) students of color on Christian college campuses.

Turning from the imagery of the doors in my own life back to the collective message we hope to convey in this chapter, both casual readers and biblical scholars have pondered the meaning and relevance of the messages to the seven churches to individual churches in the twenty-first century and to the church collectively. To the church in Philadelphia, one of two groups of believers who received affirmation and encouragement in contrast to sharp rebuke, the apostle John offers a grand vision of hope: "See, I have placed before you an open door that no one can shut" (Rev. 3:8).

In contrast to this wide-open-door message to the church in Philadelphia, a closed-door image is referenced in the words directed to the church in Laodicea. Specifically, Revelation 3:20 (one of the most well-known verses in all of Scripture) seems to target the individual rather than the collective: "Here I am! I stand at the door, and knock. If anyone hears my voice and opens the door, I will come in and eat with that person, and they with me." The image portrayed in Holman Hunt's picture (*The Light of the World*) of Jesus holding a lantern with a hand raised to rap on the rounded wooden door immediately comes to mind. Yet does that imagery accurately capture the intended meaning of the text?

Several dimensions of this verse should be noted. First, although the vast majority of sermons and Scripture-memory advocates have viewed this verse as being evangelistic (i.e., the emphasis is typically on the persistent "knocking" of a nonintrusive Savior who waits patiently to be allowed in), these words were actually directed to believers—those who already were worshipping together at Laodicea. As Mounce (1998) noted in his commentary on the book of Revelation, "In their blind self-sufficiency they had, as it were, excommunicated the risen Lord from their congregation" (p. 113). Second is the uniqueness of the Judeo-Christian tradition, among all of the world's religions, that God chooses to seek out fellowship with individuals. Third, and most directly related to the perspective offered in this chapter, is that the desired response to the knocking of God on the human heart extends beyond simply opening the door; God's desire is to enter into an intimate relationship of companionship, as symbolized through the enjoyment of a leisurely Middle Eastern meal in an atmosphere of warmth and mutual regard.

The proverbial doors of Christian higher education, as represented by the 180 campuses aligned with the CCCU, have typically not been "thrown wide open" in proactive ways that model how Christian believers value and respect the voices and perspectives of all individuals. The reasons for these shortcomings are many, including the impact of both individual and systemic sin, historical divisions and separations between the races that predate the U.S. Civil War, and the rural locations of most Christian institutions founded in the nineteenth century.

Theologically, all of the institutions represented by the CCCU are expressive in their support for kingdom priorities, which include a respect for unity among believers (John 17:20–23), love for both neighbors and strangers (Luke 10:37, Matt. 25:35), and valuing the worth and potential of each individual, anticipating the day when believers worldwide will worship together before God's throne (Rev. 7:9). In fact, many CCCU campuses are proactively opening their doors with much greater intentionality than was the case even a decade ago, both in terms of compositional "diversity" (i.e., related to demographic percentages, per Smith [2014]) and in terms of "inclusion" (i.e., referring to the respectful valuing of individuals and their diverse perspectives, per Williams [2013]). Both dimensions are important to the focus of this chapter.

Overall, the demographic trends and the explicit prioritization of diversity and inclusion on many campuses are encouraging for those who deeply desire to see Christian higher education lead the way in terms of both welcoming and serving all students well. At a national level, the CCCU and its president, Shirley V. Hoogstra, have demonstrated a commitment to diversity and racial reconciliation through a variety of initiatives. These initiatives have included the launch of a commission on diversity and inclusion; a separate track titled "Diversity and Inclusion" at the 2018 CCCU International Forum; cosponsorship of the *Diversity Matters* book project; and ongoing support of the M-E LDI initiative, involving more than seventy emerging leaders to date. Additionally, research conducted by scholars within the CCCU has focused on the factors that contribute to students of color "thriving" during the college years, with differences noted across racial and ethnic groups (McIntosh, 2012, 2015; Schreiner, 2014).

In terms of demographic trends of both students and faculty, CCCU institutions are experiencing diversification. Paralleling a trend documented by U.S. Census Bureau data that the country will have a "majority-minority" population by 2044, the percentage of students of color in the CCCU is changing, although slower than the national pace. For example, 28 percent of students at CCCU institutions as of 2014 were students of color, an increase from 19 percent in 2004 (Menjares, 2017). Even more telling, 52 CCCU institutions as of 2014 were serving a student body that was at least 28 percent students of color, and nearly half (21 campuses) had a student body reflecting 40+ percent students of color. While several indicators suggest that Christian higher education is doing a better job of welcoming and serving all students well, much work remains to be done.

The imagery of open and closed doors—and specifically the individual and collective message of Revelation 3:20 to believers, to the church, and to Christian higher education corporately—is a helpful way to frame the practical steps that can be taken to model an "ethic of care" for all students. The theological mandate for embracing this approach is also clear and compelling, with the U.S. demographic trends adding further reason for urgency. Rather than simply opening the door of access to higher education, a deep understanding of biblical hospitality is required—as exemplified in the image of offering a crackling fire and a warm home-cooked meal ("I will come in and sup with them, and they with me").

President Kim Phipps of Messiah College (PA) has, in fact, advocated the concept of hospitality as something that should permeate every aspect of campus life for Christian colleges, stating that

> Well-functioning communities nurture people through the conversations they maintain. Well-functioning communities give people the personal and emotional resources they need to flourish both as individuals *and* as persons who can help other members of the community flourish. . . . To define community in terms of mutual care and flourishing is after all a distinctively Christian, if not necessarily uniquely Christian, way of understanding the nature of community. (Phipps, 2004, pp. 172–173)

Exactly what this commitment to educating students involves can be clarified by focusing on the historical legacy of white supremacy and racism that plagues our institutions. Specifically, we need to understand the ways in which solidarity and mutuality can serve as a prism through which to envision an ethic of caring with students of color that radically transforms our communities and beloved institutions through embodied praxis. This conversation is "family talk" that demands truth-telling in love.

"Tell Those Who Plaster It Over with Whitewash"

"It is definitely because they have misled My people by saying, 'Peace!' when there is no peace. And when anyone builds a wall, behold, they plaster it over with whitewash; so tell those who plaster it over with whitewash, that it will fall" (Ezek. 13:10–11 NASB).

I (Tabatha) identify with the prophets of the Hebrew Bible because, in my personal experience, their peculiar ways of truth-telling often induce spiritual disequilibrium, which compels me to evolve. I am a black woman practitioner scholar who is embedded within the context of dominantly white (DW) Christian colleges and universities. I am also the daughter of a preacher and a minister myself. For me, the prophetic Word of God has a way of unsettling and disturbing the epistemological and hermeneutical assumptions that frame what I believe I know. In the pages that follow, I want to juxtapose the biblical imagery of doors described in the previous section with the condemnatory scene Ezekiel paints in chapter 13, where whitewashed walls are imposing and ubiquitous. Invoking the poetic symbolism of whitewashed walls in juxtaposition to open and closed doors can perhaps even more clearly illustrate the challenges facing Christian higher education and the intentional work that must be done if students of color are to experience full participation and belonging on our campuses. After all, there are doors (open or closed) and whitewashed walls in our house! In writing these words, I hope the reader will experience a deep sense of creative tension and cultural humility to empathize with what communities of color are experiencing in our institutions—places that Collins and Jun (2017) characterized as "Dominantly White Institutions (DWIs)" or dominantly white (DW) Christian colleges and universities (pp. 11–12). Taking this task to heart, I believe whitewashed walls must fall. In bringing down the walls, we can collectively witness to our loving God.

In this section of the chapter, I will first locate myself in the conversation about solidarity and mutuality with students of color. I am a student affairs practitioner-organizer at heart, so I consider it a privilege to speak directly to "my people" across a complex variety of social group identities, institutional contexts, and organizational roles. Second, I will adopt Ezekiel's imagery of whitewashed walls to problematize the structures, processes, and practices that systematically undermine solidarity and mutuality with students of color. Last, I will discuss the role that student affairs practitioners can play in embodying solidarity and mutuality with students of color. I view this approach as modeling an ethic of care that transforms

A CALLING TO CARE

institutional structures, processes, and practices through a commitment to prophetic ministry (Brueggemann, 2011).

"When and Where I Enter"

I enter this conversation in the tradition of Anna Julia Cooper, who—as a black woman and Christian educator in the U.S.—famously wrote in 1892, "when and where I enter, in the quiet, undisputed dignity of my womanhood, without violence and without suing or special patronage, then and there the whole Negro race enters with me" (p. 30). While the goal of the chapter is to imagine an ethic of care that expresses solidarity and mutuality with students of color and transforms DW Christian colleges and universities, I want to first make visible some of my own identities, because they shape my perspectives as a practitioner scholar. Situating myself within this conversation is, of course, a paradox. I do not pretend to represent all black people, all people of color, or all women of color in the academy. At the same time, by exhibiting self-reflectivity, I hope to inspire student affairs practitioners toward a commitment to self-reflective practice that identifies and challenges the interlocking systems of oppression that function asymmetrically across our institutions to harm communities of color. The invitation to self-reflectivity, solidarity, and mutuality involves reimagining with communities of color new possibilities and ways of being that can transform Christian higher education in life-giving ways. I view this emancipatory and deeply spiritual work as being central to the calling God has placed upon my life.

Presently, I teach doctoral students in higher education at Azusa Pacific University, and prior to this role, I spent nearly twenty years as an educational leader and student affairs practitioner-organizer at Pepperdine University. I have served in roles such as associate dean of student affairs, Title IX coordinator, and associate vice president for student life. I have also provided strategic oversight and guidance to key student-life areas, such as campus recreation, chapel and student-led ministries, residential life, student activities, volunteer, career, and student employment services, and diversity and inclusion programs. Among the university-wide committees

126

I chaired were diversity councils and student care teams. I have also been principally engaged in institutional transformation efforts that focus on diversity, equity, and inclusion as a paradigm through which to enact justice and educational excellence. For me, this paradigm is a conceptual and theological one that calls me to center the experiences of minoritized communities of color in the reimagination of institutional flourishing.

As a black woman whose professional career has been cultivated in DWIs, I identify with how sociologist Patricia Hill Collins (1986) described the "outsider within" (p. 514) status black women occupy in society and academe. Among the multiple dimensions of my identity, for example, I am a churched Christian whose documented status as a U.S. citizen, high level of educational attainment, dominant-ability status, and linguistic background function together to confer social capital and privileged status ("within" status), and a sense of familiarity with the cultures of the Christian academy. In this way, I benefit from unearned advantage through insider knowledge, dispositions, and skills that I activate with ease. Simultaneously, as a black woman in higher education, I am often rendered invisibly visible as an "outsider" and "other." This happens in subtle and overt ways. In Christian DWIs, my minoritized racial and gender identities are salient, pronounced, and acute. Despite the unearned privileges from which I benefit, my minoritized social group status as a black woman is tokenizing, othering, and dispossessing—what James Baldwin explicated when adopting the proverbial saying "fly in buttermilk" as the title of a short story about a black male teen attending an all-white school (as cited in Baldwin & Morrison, 1998, pp. 187–196).

Otherness in contrast to dominance or normativity must be understood not only in interpersonal terms but also in relationship to power and the interlocking systems of oppression (Hill Collins, 1986) at work in institutions. Without critical awareness and understanding of what Barbara Smith referred to as the "simultaneity of oppression" (as cited in Hill Collins, 1986, p. 519), interpersonal and institutional care efforts "for" students of color can unwittingly devolve into a form of white savior paternalism. Moreover, subtle and overt forces which demand that communities of color assimilate and conform to white dominant norms are alive in every aspect of institutional life, and dominant whiteness as a system is unrelenting in its grasp on power, which functions culturally, structurally, religiously, and in embodied ways.

As a "fly in buttermilk" (as cited in Baldwin & Morrison, 1998, pp. 187–196), I have routinely been the only person of color at decision-making tables in university settings. Simultaneously, the overrepresentation of patriarchal whiteness has remained intact. The minoritization of communities of color and overrepresentation of white folks not only diminish our collective potential but also erode our collective capacity to witness to God's presence in the world and the kinship to which we are called through the gospel. Moreover, the institutional pattern of overreliance upon a marginal presence of a few people of color to "diversify" institutions tokenizes the multidimensional voices of communities of color and systematically reinforces patriarchal whiteness. When people of color are tokenized in institutions, a culture of assimilation that privileges white dominant norms is prevalent. In this way, I believe patriarchal whiteness is at work in idolatrous ways within our institutions.

While the sacrifices of many people across interracial lines made possible the dismantling of the U.S. racial apartheid system, the process is a continual one within our institutions and society. After all, white dominance (Collins & Jun, 2017) still manifests in peculiar ways. For example, I have been the first black woman or person of color to serve in a number of administrative capacities. This reality is not something to celebrate. It is 2018. It is not uncommon for students and employees to tell me that I am their first professor or supervisor of color. Moreover, I have observed how the vast contributions of black women and other communities of color to knowledge production and educational practice are continually erased or marginalized. I agree with Delgado Bernal and Villalpando (2002), who asserted that the devaluing of the multiple forms of knowledge that communities of color produce is an example of the "apartheid of knowledge" that persists in academe through "epistemological racism" (p. 169).

The invisible forms of labor people of color contribute to the academy are frequently devalued in formalized evaluation and promotion systems. It is from the vantage point of an "outsider within" (Hill Collins, 1986) that I closely identify with the multiple ways students of color might experience Christian DWIs. And still, students of color experience institutions in ways that are vastly different from my own. Nonetheless, this doubly proximate and marginal viewpoint—a peculiar location, to be sure—compels me toward urgent reflection about the legacy of patriarchal white supremacy and racism that plagues higher education institutions—including those imbued with Christian purposes.

For black women who labor in the higher education system, the acute visibility and invisibility we experience in dominantly white spaces is instructive in illuminating the structural conditions that reproduce patriarchal whiteness, but it also induces the kind of creative imagination that might lead to greater critical consciousness and life-giving praxis with students of color.

Christian colleges and universities, after all, are not neutral spaces. Without being consciously aware, we can unwittingly sustain structures of death—whitewashed walls that symbolically represent forces that undermine the agency and humanity of students of color and white folks—and diminish the presence of God.

While this kind of truth-telling may induce discomfort or denial, I have come to believe that central to imagining an ethic of care with students of color in DW Christian colleges and universities is the need to name, challenge, and confront the closed doors and whitewashed walls in our institutions. This task is a particularly challenging one since ideologies and systems of patriarchal white supremacy can masquerade as biblical logic. Nonetheless, I agree with Cornel West, who says repeatedly, "Justice is what love looks like in public." I also believe in the remarkable potential of Christian colleges and universities, and student affairs professionals working in that context, to disrupt the ways in which dominant systems and ideologies of patriarchal whiteness function to sustain privilege and power. Building our collective capacity to "see" and describe reality as it is will be essential to the reimagining and collective transformation of our institutions.

"When Anyone Builds a Wall"

> "The pastoral reality is that this ideology of privilege sustained by power is so pervasive that it is the air we breathe and the water in which we swim. It is beyond question or criticism; it renders us incapable of thinking or imagining outside of its definitions of reality" (Brueggemann, 2011, p. 4).

Although Brueggemann (2011) in the preceding quote described the ideologies of imperialism and militarism that permeate U.S. culture, the description "privilege sustained by power is so pervasive that it is the air we breathe and the water in which we swim" is also a useful depiction of the white architecture of DWIs (Collins & Jun, 2017). In Ahmed's (2012) research study of diversity practitioners in colleges and universities, participants frequently described how their experiences with the forces of resistance to diversity work in institutions felt like "banging your head against a brick wall" (p. 26). Like participants in Ahmed's study, I have observed a number of ways in which students of color at DWIs encounter whitewashed brick walls and experience "coming up against something that does not move, something solid and tangible" (p. 26). By describing my own observations, my goal is not to indict a single institution. Rather, I hope to incite deep and continuous reflection about the myriad of ways DW Christian colleges and universities in the contemporary era maintain doors that are closed (unknowingly or deliberately) and walls that are whitewashed.

After all, the systems and ideologies of patriarchal whiteness are socially engineered. Nonetheless, these phenomena have extraordinary theological, ideological, psychological, legal, and embodied consequences for communities of color and white people. Although patriarchal whiteness as an ideology is often tacit, normative, assumed, and hidden to its beneficiaries, it is omnipresent, overrepresented, and ubiquitous to communities of color, who are underrepresented, minoritized, marginalized, and hypervisible in DWIs. The widely-used framework for diversity that Smith (2009) developed is a useful tool to inspire institutional reflection and action that considers the systemic dimensions of diversity, namely, "climate and intergroup relations, education and scholarship, access and success, institutional viability and vitality" (p. 243). Smith's framework is also beneficial to reflective processes that consider how patriarchal whiteness is sustained and reinforced, so that we can work proactively and intentionally disrupt it. In celebrating the laudable efforts at work in CCCU schools to make diversity, equity, and inclusion matter (Longman, 2017), I want to simultaneously invite reflection about everyday experiences in student life that illustrate the stubborn stronghold of whitewashed walls. My goal is not to discredit the good work already underway. Instead, I hope to inspire a sustained and relentless commitment to self-appraisal and action among student affairs professionals in ways that will fuel counter-imagination with students of color to collectively and courageously enact institutional renewal and transformation.

Whitewashed Brick Walls in Student Life

Below, I provide four examples to situate the discussion about whitewashed walls within the context of student life. I apply the interrelated dimensions of Smith's (2009) framework for diversity to organize the examples. The patterns I describe are not an exhaustive list of concerns. Instead, I have included them to encourage critical thinking and reflection about the complex issues facing Christian higher education across a myriad of institutions, roles, and departments.

"Institutional Viability and Vitality"

Smith (2009) provided a number of indicators to signal the "capacity-building" nature of the "institutional viability and vitality" dimension and emphasized the connection to "vitality" (p. 247). In student life, one obvious concern is the hiring and retention of a diverse staff team that is committed to diversity, equity, inclusion, and critical consciousness. This concern applies not only to professional staff teams but also to the selection of student leaders, such as resident advisers and orientation ambassadors.

The persistence of majority-white staff teams is concerning, especially when taken together with the phenomenon of white overrepresentation in university leadership, faculty, board membership, and the student body. The enduring pattern—the overrepresentation of white women and men and their proximity to institutional power (e.g., control of financial resources, curriculum, policy development)—is drastically misaligned with our institutional missions, visions, and stated commitments to diversity. Moreover, teams in student affairs assume liability when recruitment and hiring processes do not identify in prospective candidates the critical consciousness, capacity, and skills needed to maximize the educational benefits of diversity through culturally relevant pedagogy.

"Education and Scholarship"

Curricular transformation has been at the center of student protests since the 1960s and their resurgence across a number of U.S. campuses in the last two years. In acts of "creative protest" (King, 1960, p. 367), students of color have registered nonviolent public dissent about the pace and quality of curricular transformation and demanded more inclusive curricula. Although Smith (2009) framed the "education and scholarship" (pp. 247–248) domain exclusively in terms of the formal curriculum and the faculty's capacity to contribute to inclusive scholarship, I would add that the formal and informal cocurriculum for which student affairs is responsible must also be examined. New student orientation, leadership development, student activities, and chapel programs often reflect a normative cultural ethos of patriarchal whiteness. Student-led activities, campus traditions, missions, self-governance structures, and living environments often reflect similar norms. When the curriculum and cocurriculum conform to a pervasive "White racial logic" (Zuberi & Bonilla-Silva, 2008, p. 4), patriarchal whiteness is automatically reproduced. This process creates a toxic atmosphere for everyone, especially communities of color. Critical race scholars Lani Guinier and Gerald Torres (2003) drew a powerful connection between the metaphor of the miner's canary and the nature of race and racism in the context of social environments:

Those who are racially marginalized are like the miner's canary: their distress is the first sign of a danger that threatens us all. It is easy enough to think that when we sacrifice the canary, the only harm is to communities of color. Yet others ignore problems that converge around racial minorities at their own peril, for these problems are symptoms warning us all. (p. 11)

In the dynamic context of contemporary student activism, university communities should ask, "What might we learn from and with activist students of color, and how might centering their voices and concerns transform our institutions in ways that more deeply fulfill our missions?"

Campus "Climate and Intergroup Relations"

The prevalence of microaggressions and racist incidents on campus— whether they occur in residence halls or classrooms—is an indicator of "climate and intergroup relations" (Smith, 2009, pp. 249–250). The alarming nature of these episodes can obscure the institutional reality that too few campuses invest adequate financial, staffing, and organizational resources to effectively lead and empower institutional transformation. While isolated incidents are particularly distressing emergencies for people of color in university communities, it is also true that communities of color experience the magnitude of everyday encounters with patriarchal whiteness, which is embedded within the architecture, institutional histories, and administration of colleges and universities. This, too, is an equally urgent concern that must be addressed with the same kind of institutional vigilance that gets applied to episodic incidents. Without proper institutional vision, capacity, leadership, and resources, the work of diversity and transformation often falls to the goodwill of a few students, faculty, and staff of color.

"Access and Success"

Making meaning of institutional data on a routine basis to understand "access and success" (Smith, 2009, pp. 250–251) in disaggregated ways is a critical priority. Yet, the nature and pace of the work in student life can make this responsibility particularly difficult. Perhaps emotional fatigue and burnout are symptoms of "academic capitalism" (Slaughter & Rhoades, 2010, p. 1), the multiple processes by which colleges and universities engage the global economy. The emotional labor and workload associated with realities such as crisis response is a seemingly impenetrable wall. Smith (2009) framed the "access and success" (p. 250) domain in terms of basic indicators, such as GPA and graduation, but also asked whether students of color "are *thriving* at the institution" (p. 250). Efforts in student affairs to ensure thriving can only be understood through a continual process of meaning-making that disaggregates institutional data about the student experience. However, a commitment to critical meaning-making requires time and energy for sustained, deliberate, and culturally relevant reflection. Demands in student affairs often leave professionals without the bandwidth to engage in reflective meaning-making practices.

Solidarity and Mutuality as an Ethic of Care

Returning to the influence of the prophets, actualizing the belief that students of color matter in theory, policy, and practice within Christian colleges and universities will demand that student affairs practitioners develop the capacity for prophetic ministry. Brueggemann (2011) posited that the prophetic tradition "aimed to *reimagine the world as though the character of YHWH were a real and lively and engaged agent in the world*" (p. 3, emphasis original). Communities that hold closely to the belief and knowledge of God's presence in the world must recognize that

> In our own context where denial is the order of the day, the prophetic ministry of truth-telling exposes the euphemisms that disguise and calls things by their right name. Prophetic faith is propelled by pain, the pain that greed imposes on the vulnerable, the pain that violence propagates on those at risk. It requires a noticing eye and a suffering tongue to call attention to the deep hurt that is inflicted on some by others, by policy, by indiffer-ence, by self-assertiveness at the expense of the neighbor, all of which contradict the rule of YHWH. (p. 12)

For Brueggemann, the prophetic ministry of truth-telling is only possible because God's presence in the world is real. In this way, God is the ultimate source of prophetic ministry, and only God makes possible solidarity and mutuality in *"truth and hope"* (p. 21).

From my vantage point as a practitioner scholar, I want to share what I have learned (and continue to learn) during my career in college student affairs from and with hundreds of students of color and white-majority students whose prophetic ministry of solidarity and mutuality has radically altered my life. I offer these suggestions as a starting point to encourage student affairs practitioners to invest in a continuous process of self-reflection, reimagination, and collective action in solidarity and mutuality with God, students of color, white-majority students, and other members of the university community, such as faculty, campus leaders, board members, alumni, advancement partners, and the public—local and global—to which we are called to engage and serve.

Embodied Care and Praxis

In the foreword to Paulo Freire's critical work *Pedagogy of the Oppressed*, Richard Shaull asserted that systems of education either reinforce "conformity" to the status quo or facilitate "the practice of freedom" (as cited in Freire, 2007, p. 34). Transformation takes root as a practice of freedom, an embodied process of action and reflection that is grounded in love and cultivates critical consciousness (Freire, 2007; hooks, 2000). Love is an animating, enlivening, and "transformative force" (hooks, 2000, p. xix). Solidarity and mutuality, then, can first be understood through the biblical command to love God and neighbor as one's self. It is God's love that frees us in Jesus and through the work of the Spirit to bear witness to the kinship Jesus embodies. Striving to imitate Jesus in the fullness of our humanity is at the center of a prophetic ministry of solidarity and mutuality. Moreover, Freire (2007) contended, "Liberation is a praxis: the action and reflection of men and women upon their world in order to transform it" (p. 79). Praxis involves a commitment to the humanity of others and one's self, and it is cultivated through a regular practice of self-reflectivity and a posture of cultural humility—"a lifelong process of self-reflection, self-critique, continual assessment of power imbalances, and the development of mutually respectful relationships and partnerships" (Gallardo, 2013, p. 3).

Critical Tools and Strategies

Critical tools and strategies also enhance praxis. Black women scholars first theorized about the function of "intersectionality" as an analytical strategy to make visible the interlocking systems of oppression that communities of color traverse (Crenshaw, 1991; Hill Collins, 1986). By naming, challenging, and confronting intersectional forms of oppression (e.g., ability, gender, race, ethnicity, immigration status, social class), student affairs professionals can more clearly align student affairs theory, policy, and practices with beliefs about students as fully human and capable of asserting their own agency. Centering the multiplicity of voices and lived experiences among students of color can also interrupt essentialist thinking. This centering means inviting diverse communities of students to decision-making tables in student affairs and at the highest levels of the institution, particularly in the development of new policy and practice. It also means that students must have an equitable stake in driving institutional agendas. Moreover, when adopting "inclusive and differentiated" (Smith, 2009, p. 79) approaches to institutional care, student affairs professionals must recognize the multiple dimensions of diversity in students' lives while also "differentiating" (p. 79) where attention should be focused. Although it is common sense, it is worth mentioning, for example, that undocumented students of color have equally important but very different needs from students of color with disabilities.

Levers for Systemic Change

In terms of systemic change, I want to highlight four areas in which to invest effort and resources. Developing faculty-staff-student partnerships that encourage seamless learning across the curriculum and cocurriculum is an important way to demonstrate solidarity and mutuality. One such example is a sophomore experience program our team developed at Pepperdine. The dynamic process of imagining, designing, and executing an educational trip to San Francisco during the Martin Luther King Jr. holiday for students, faculty, staff, and their families to explore social movement histories in the region has proven to be a rich laboratory for learning. Rather than working in silos, we convened students, faculty, and student affairs staff at the design table. Students, after all, do not experience the institution in the fragmented ways to which we can become accustomed.

Another lever for change is the development and ongoing improvement of university-wide student care teams. Teams should reflect compositional and ideological diversity, as well as participation across the full span of institutional care. High-functioning student care teams are a vehicle for campus change in policy and practice, particularly when student needs and sense of agency are placed at the center.

Investing in the Work

Institutions must also invest financial, staffing, and organizational resources to prevent the overreliance upon students of color to perform cultural trans-formation work that institutions should provide. The persistent challenges of constrained budgets and understaffed diversity and inclusion offices must also be redressed. Similarly, student affairs professionals can ensure that the governance structures for student organizations equitably allocate resources. This allocation ensures that organizations which students of color form can persist. Finally, student affairs divisions must ensure the routine and effective delivery of professional development programs for professionals and student teams. Developing organizational capacity for critical con-sciousness, knowledge, and skills development across student affairs teams *and* in close proximity with students of color is an important way to make reflection, truth-telling, and reimagination the norm.

A Call to Action

As we bring the chapter to a close, we invite you as colleagues to join us in accepting a call to action—the practice of prophetic ministry. We return to a biblical vision of hope that reminds us of God's agency in the world: "See, I have placed before you an open door that no one can shut" (Rev. 3:8). It is God's active presence in the world that frees us as communities within Christian colleges and universities to bear witness to the kinship of God, which always opens doors and removes whitewashed walls. In solidarity and mutuality with students of color as our full partners, it is our prayer that student affairs professionals will leverage their influence in intentional and proactive ways to shape the institutional agendas, conditions, and pathways toward change. We invite you to join us in the ongoing task of reimagining our collective potential to bear witness to the kin-dom of God, "on earth as it is in heaven" (Matt. 6:10).

We also want to encourage student affairs professionals in "truth and hope" (Brueggemann, 2011, p. 21) to consider how we might collectively witness to God's presence in the world through a prophetic ministry of mutuality and solidarity with students of color. We believe this task compels us to open closed doors, to transform the whitewashed walls that dehumanize us, and to practice hospitality in ways that reveal the life-giving nature of the gospel.

References

Ahmed, S. (2012). *On being included: Racism and diversity in institutional life.* Durham, NC: Duke University Press.

Baldwin, J., & Morrison, T. (1998). *Baldwin: Collected essays.* New York, NY: Literary Classics.

Brueggemann, W. (2011). Prophetic leadership: Engagement in counter-imagination. *Journal of Religious Leadership, 10*(1), 1–23. Retrieved from http://bit.ly/2rqFXSl

Collins, C. S., & Jun, A. (2017). *White out: Understanding white privilege and dominance in the modern age.* New York, NY: Peter Lang.

Cooper, A. J. (1892). *A voice from the South.* Xenia, OH: Aldine Printing House.

Council for Christian Colleges & Universities. (2015, March 2). CCCU launches commission on diversity and inclusion. Retrieved from https://www.cccu .org/news/articles/2015/Diversity Commission

Crenshaw, K. (1991). Mapping the margins: Intersectionality, identity politics, and violence against women of color. *Stanford Law Review, 43,* 1241–1299. Retrieved from http://www.bwjp.org/assets/mapping-the-margins-crenshaw .pdf

Delgado Bernal, D., & Villalpando, O. (2002). An apartheid of knowledge in academia: The struggle over the "legitimate" knowledge of faculty of color. *Equity & Excellence in Education, 35,* 169–180. doi:10.1080/713845282

Freire, P. (2007). *Pedagogy of the oppressed* (30th ed.). New York, NY: Continuum International Publishing Group.

Gallardo, M. (2013). *Developing cultural humility: Embracing race, privilege and power.* Thousand Oaks, CA: SAGE Publications.

Guinier, L., & Torres, G. (2003). *The miner's canary: Enlisting race, resisting power, transforming democracy.* Cambridge, MA: Harvard University Press.

Hill Collins, P. (1986). Learning from the outsider within: The sociological significance of black feminist thought. *Social Problems, 33,* 514–532. doi:10.2307/800672

hooks, b. (2000). *All about love: New visions.* New York, NY: William Morrow.

King, M. L. (1960). *A creative protest* [Transcript]. Retrieved from http://okra .stanford.edu/transcription/document_images/Vol05Scans/16Feb1960 _ACreativeProtest.pdf

Longman, K. A. (Ed.). (2017). *Diversity matters: Race, ethnicity, and the future of Christian higher education.* Abilene, TX: Abilene Christian University Press.

McIntosh, E. J. (2012). *Thriving in college: The role of spirituality and psychological sense of community in students of color* (Doctoral dissertation). Retrieved from ProQuest Dissertations and Theses. (Order No. 3521901)

McIntosh, E. J. (2015). Thriving and spirituality: Making meaning of meaning making for students of color. *About Campus, 19*(6), 16–23. doi:10.1002 /abc.21175

Menjares, P. C. (2017). Diversity in the CCCU: The current state and implications for the future. In K. A. Longman (Ed.), *Diversity matters: Race, ethnicity, and the future of Christian higher education* (pp. 11–30). Abilene, TX: Abilene Christian University Press.

Mounce, R. H. (1998). *The book of Revelation.* Grand Rapids, MI: Eerdmans.

Phipps, K. (2004). Epilogue: Campus climate and Christian scholarship. In D. Jacobsen & R. H. Jacobsen (Eds.), *Scholarship and Christian faith: Enlarging the conversation* (pp. 171–183). New York, NY: Oxford University Press.

Pohl, C. D. (1999). *Making room: Recovering hospitality as a Christian tradition.* Grand Rapids, MI: Eerdmans.

Schreiner, L. A. (2014). Different pathways to thriving among students of color: An untapped opportunity for success. *About Campus, 19*(5), 10–19. doi:10.1002/abc.21169

Slaughter, S., & Rhoades, G. (2010). *Academic capitalism and the new economy: Markets, state, and higher education.* Baltimore, MD: Johns Hopkins University Press.

Smith, D. G. (2009). *Diversity's promise for higher education: Making it work.* Baltimore, MD: Johns Hopkins University Press.

Smith, D. G. (2014). *Diversity and inclusion in higher education: Emerging perspectives on institutional transformation.* Abingdon, UK: Routledge.

Williams, D. A. (2013). *Strategic diversity leadership: Activating change and transformation in higher education.* Sterling, VA: Stylus Publishing.

Zuberi, T., & Bonilla-Silva, E. (Eds.). (2008). *White logic, white methods: Racism and methodology.* Lanham, MD: Rowman & Littlefield Publishers.

7

CALL(S) AND CARE(S) IN COLLEGIATE MINISTRY

DONALD D. OPITZ

Messiah College

I imagine that some kind of Christian ministry for college students takes place on every college and university campus in the United States and on most campuses around the world. The models of ministry are as diverse as the campuses and the students that they serve. Some campuses are served by one or more church-based ministries, and most of these programs seek to integrate students more fully into the life of a congregation. Other campuses are served by one or more parachurch ministry organizations. These groups display various theological emphases and ministry strategies. Ministry that is sanctioned and supported by the college or university often takes place through a particular office served by college pastors, priests, or chaplains. On smaller church-related campuses, these programs are likely shaped by the institution's founding tradition, but on many campuses these programs are multidenominational or multifaith collaborations. There are also student-led ministry initiatives that may have nothing to do with a local church, parachurch leaders, or institutional oversight. The roles, resources, goals, and strategies of all these ministries vary with the local context of each program and with the theological vision that drives the ministry.

This chapter explores a theology of caring and calling that might inform any of these models and inspire fresh collaboration. The following section places these ideas of caring and calling into a biblical context. The contours and dynamics of collegiate ministry are then discussed in the ensuing sections: Student Care, Pastoral Care, Soul Care, and Student Cares.

Caring and Calling in Biblical Context

Sometimes we use the word *care* to mean something like *concern* or *worry*, as in "I don't have a care in the world," or as in Psalm 55:22: "Cast your cares on the LORD and he will sustain you." That conception aligns well with the Saxon origins of the word—to feel concern about something, even to the point of worry. In a Christian context, care has taken on warmer connotations, reaching beyond concern to compassion. When we say that we care about someone, we often mean that we cherish them and that we will attend to them and support them. This care is rooted in and infused with love. The love that fuels care is (in the quartet of Greek variations on love) not the *eros* of sexual attraction, or the *philia* of friendship, or the familial love of *storge*. Care is an expression of the *agape* of God that flows to us and through us to others. Love's source is the God of love, and its end is to see the recipient hale and whole. Caring for students is not simply displaying concern, and it is not mere sentimentality. It is agape love, a love that nudges the recipient toward wholeness. When we care, we are doing our best to imitate God and to love our neighbors.

In the final post-resurrection story in John 21, Jesus stands on the shore of the Sea of Galilee. The disciples have been fishing all night long without success. Jesus (the disciples don't know that it is him yet) shouts to them to try the other side of the boat. They do, and the net strains with 153 large fish. Peter realizes that it is Jesus, and he leaps into the water to swim to his master and friend. Jesus already has breakfast on the fire, and he invites the disciples to enjoy it with him. After breakfast Jesus has a hard talk with Peter. He asks Peter three times, "Do you love me?" And with increasing intensity Peter (who had denied knowing Christ three times) affirms his love. And each time Jesus indicates the path of love—care for my sheep and follow me. Peter doesn't forget this lesson. He later reminds church elders that Jesus is the chief shepherd and that they are "shepherds of God's flock that is under [their] care" (1 Pet. 5:1–4).

Ministry begins in love. Jesus called out and Peter jumped in. The gospel is an invitation to jump into the love of the Trinity—to discover the love of the Father, the grace of the Lord Jesus, and the fellowship of the Holy Spirit. After stepping into the love of God, followers step out to share the abundant love they have received. Collegiate ministry begins in love, and it is expressed in love and in the care of students and colleagues.

God is love, and the persons of the Trinity are engaged in mutual and everlasting love that was opened up to include church and creation. Every act of human love is made possible by the God who created the human capacity for love and extended a history in which love could be expressed amid the ruins of sin. The extent of God's love was displayed in God's willingness to become incarnate—embodied in and covenanted to the creation forevermore. That same love was displayed on the cross—that God's love would overcome any obstacle, no matter the cost. And the love of God for church and creation continues to be poured out through Christ Jesus and by the agency of the Holy Spirit, and mediately through the faithful witness of the caring ambassadors God has called and equipped. God's strong love restores through Christ Jesus, and the kingdom is the *telos* of that redeeming love. Collegiate ministry has the same telos, and the calls of the Lord reveal the end the Lord has in view.

While caring has become a love-pregnant word, calling, on the other hand, has been emptied of nuance and power in contemporary usage. This biblical idea, once packed with meaning, has been hijacked to serve other slim purposes. In medieval Europe, to be called meant to be called out of everyday life and culture into ecclesial duty or monastic orders. A few were called, but most were not. In modern context, calling is invariably a summons to work in some particular field or at a particular job. Students pick up on this definition and generally take calling and vocation to mean the same thing as career and job. In this modern context, calling becomes a useful (though limited) notion to encourage young professionals to find their place in the overwhelming thrall of the modern marketplace. Once a student chooses a path through the thicket of options, "calling" has been resolved, and a happy life on the other side of calling's anxiety can begin. The dynamic biblical ideas of a living God who calls and the rich spirituality of discerning the caller's messages have been largely lost.

In the biblical drama, calling is deep and wide. It is as deep as the *vox deus* itself—God's creation-ordering, life-directing, and love-delivering Word. It is revealed in the very first chapter of the Bible when God calls creation into being, and we hear it in the very last chapter as the ascended Christ reminds readers he is returning soon. Throughout the Bible, God calls again and again. Human purpose is framed by God's calls to stewardship, cultural development, and missional proclamation. God's voice is heard in the whispers of wisdom and in the thunder of storm and sea. God's character and restorative purposes are revealed to redemptive heroes as well as through the preaching and writing of prophets and apostles as they testify on God's behalf. Along the coast of Galilee, Jesus calls the disciples, and disciples are still being called by the ongoing work of God's Spirit. Those people who hear the call can't help but call back in praise of the One whose word is life and whose way is love.

The Bible is the book of callings. Discerning which calls are relevant and how to live faithfully in response to those calls requires dynamic engagement with this book of calls and the God who calls. Such engagement has led to various Christian traditions, and there is much to learn from the insights and practices of many of these traditions—Jesuit, Pietist, Lutheran, Puritan, Wesleyan, and Neo-Calvinist, to name a few (Placher, 2005). One insight that has helped me and that I think students need to learn is that while the call of the Lord can be specific and personal, it is most often general and communal. The Lord may call an individual to take on an assignment (build an ark, lead the exodus, confront a king), go to a certain place (Sidon, Nineveh, Macedonia), or fill a particular office (priest, elder, parent). As a college student, I longed to hear the voice of the Lord. I think I wanted to know my life mattered (the gospel should be assurance enough for that), and I wanted to know I was following the narrow path of obedience. While I do believe the Lord provides precise guidance for some, most of us will choose (prayerfully, of course) between many good options—artist or astronaut, Pittsburgh or Pakistan, single or married. Many students share the same decision-making agony that I did, assuming that calling is precise and that God will communicate directly—if not audibly—if only they are worthy.

Attention to the consistent and common calls of the Lord—those calls that shape the contours of faithful life in God's world—can help to relieve the anxiety so many students experience, and it can invite students into the communal pursuit of faithfulness. An important part of the work of collegiate ministry is to help students come to know God's character and intentions by giving attention to these revealed calls. Most of the Christian life is defined not by unique calls, but by the general calls of the Lord. God calls us:

- to work and be creative, as well as to rest and celebrate;
- to honor our parents;
- to be truthful;
- to seek justice and to defend the oppressed;
- to cherish wisdom;
- to be good stewards of the creation, our resources, and our time;
- to develop Christian character;
- to bear witness near and far;
- to follow Christ as an obedient disciple; and
- to love God and neighbor with all we have.

A robust and biblical theology of calling reveals the nature and will of God and invites us to attend to the caller. It also reveals that the Christian life is framed by callings and fulfilled by faithful response to God's multiple calls. We will return to the rich array of calls in the final section of this chapter.

So far I have simply argued that care is really love and that call is really calls. These points are two key pillars for a contextual and collaborative strategy for collegiate ministry.

Student Care

College ministry is the work of loving college students and helping them to discern the multiple calls of the Lord, and this process takes time. There are many reasons why the pace of ministry is slow. There are numerous obstacles—practical, cultural, and spiritual. But the key reason ministry is slow is that it was designed to be slow; it was designed to take place in relationships and at the pace of relationships. Kosuke Koyama (1980) made this argument in a most memorable way in *Three Mile an Hour God*. Jesus invested three years in ministry, and he invested in a limited number of disciples. He taught and healed at various locations around the Sea of Galilee and then, in the final months of ministry, in Judea and finally Jerusalem. His work with the disciples took place at these events and around the campfire, and often the disciples were coached on the road while walking. Jesus engaged in discipleship at three mph—not hurrying to the next encounter, not distracted by the vast needs and opportunities that pressed in on him. His pace was casual—ambulation that fostered conversation. Transformational ministry unfolds in relationships, and relationships take time.

Because the pace is slow, ministry requires a team. It is done best when a team of colleagues and student leaders works together. Ideally, everyone who works for a college or university loves not only students but also learning. College ministry staff share with other educational colleagues a vocation driven by the love of students and the love of learning. This shared love does not mean that faculty, administrators, and staff will have the experience, skills, or desire to be involved in ministry, but some will. Creating a diverse and dynamic team takes time and effort, and this pace is the essence of collaborative ministry.

Several decades ago, it was not uncommon for the chaplain or dean of religious life at small Christian and church-related colleges to serve on the president's cabinet with other campus leaders. These clerical representatives often stood for the interests of the founding denomination and added theological and ministerial perspective. It is now much more common to find an office of college ministry—if one exists at all—under the umbrella of student affairs. While this change may reflect a loss of status and influence, it provides a great opportunity for input among a division of peers who are committed to caring for students in various ways. If the division of student affairs rises above managerial and cocurricular concerns to engage key educational outcomes (e.g., identity formation, purpose formation, social formation, academic formation, faith/spiritual formation), wise leaders can help to provide a theological or spiritual perspective for each of these aims.

The student affairs division may play a strategic role in teaching educators about the ever-changing students that quickly cycle through the academy. In order to love college students, we have to know them. At many institutions, admissions and student affairs collaborate to provide a state-of-the-student address. Who is coming to college, and in particular who is coming to this college? New colleagues and veteran faculty may be surprised to learn about changing student demographics. Educators may also benefit from guided reflection on the changing hopes and beliefs of students. What are their financial aspirations? How many indicate interest in civic matters or service opportunities? Why are they coming to college? What religious beliefs and practices do they report?

Student affairs professionals should also be equipped to help educators understand the transitional challenges of students. We would be wise to eschew many of the labels for this age cohort that have been coined—extended adolescence is better than "adultesence" or "kidult," but not much better. Perhaps the most helpful label was coined by Jeffrey Arnett (2004). He referred to those people between 18 and 30 years of age as *emerging adults*. These novice adults are wrestling with various "coming of age" challenges in our culture, and those challenges are perceived differently than they were several decades ago. Instead of coming to view adulthood as taking on responsibilities like marriage and parenting, the new adulthood is achieved once educational and professional goals are met and economic independence is earned. Emerging adulthood is viewed as an extended period of *becoming* in which young adults wrestle with identity formation, purpose formation, relationship formation, academic formation, and faith formation. Helpful theories, models, and best practices have been developed for each of these transformational aims.

Chaplains ought to have constructive contributions to make to help students through each of these transformational challenges, but without their input on faith formation, this aspect of human development may be set aside. James Fowler's (1981, 1987, 2000) theory regarding stages of faith could be explored, and insight regarding its limitations and applications could be discussed (Andrade, 2014; Astley & Francis, 1992; Dykstra & Parks, 1986). Fowler's stages could be laid alongside James Marcia's (1993) identity theory to generate fruitful insights regarding student readiness for growth. Faith development theory has already been constructively connected to ministry and counseling modalities for fostering student growth (Lindholm, Mallorca, Schwartz, & Spinoza, 2011; Parker, 2011; Parks, 2000; Stanard & Painter, 2004).

Robert Wuthnow's (1998) sociological analysis of American spirituality in the latter half of the twentieth century has obvious implications for ministerial care for college students. He discusses a spirituality of dwelling, which anchors the person to place and tradition, as well as a spirituality of seeking, which readies the spiritual sojourner for the road. Since both forms of spirituality are deeply rooted in the biblical text and revisited by various traditions, it makes sense for us to introduce students to both dimensions of Christian faithfulness. Christian faithfulness is formed through investment in the here and now as well as preparation for wherever and whenever. Students who are ready to grow are like good clay—they are not soupy, nor are they hardened. When students are anchored and exploring, healthy growth can be fostered. Wuthnow (2007) also explored characteristics of the faith of emerging adults, outlining the opportunities and challenges facing the church and educational institutions that hope to guide faith development.

The compelling work of Christian Smith cannot be ignored. Smith and Denton (2009) introduced readers to the dominant presence of moralistic therapeutic deism (MTD) among American youth, and they lamented the failure of youth ministry programs and the educational programs of churches. Smith and Snell (2009) followed up that research, turning their attention to emerging adults. They showed that the collegiate spiritual landscape is also dominated by MTD. College ministry programs are going to need to work hard to combat moralism with a theology of grace, replace therapeutic self-help with deep discipleship, and guide students beyond deism into rich and living relationship with the Triune God of Christian orthodoxy. Setran and Kiesling (2013) attended to this challenge in *Spiritual Formation in Emerging Adulthood*.

We must do our homework to know our students. Doing this homework together builds common ground and collegiality. The goal, of course, is not merely to know about students, but it is to come to know them, and that process is not easy. Forging the relationship requires openness and initiative. Both parties need to be open to the relationship, but students are busy and so are college administrators, educators, and ministers. Some students will shrink from friendship with an administrator due to age variance or with a chaplain due to an allergic reaction to the collar (whether you are wearing one or not). Even if you are winsome and gregarious, something else may stand in the way—*pain*. Many students come to college hurt, and many will be hurt during the college years.

Pastoral Care

Tom Wolfe's (2004) *I Am Charlotte Simmons: A Novel* unmasked brutal aspects of U.S. university life. The damage and pain endured by the title character are heartbreaking. All students hurt a little, but some hurt all the time, and deeply. Knowing college students means we need to know their pain. Poor Charlotte broke my heart, and the pain of college students breaks my heart too. I will provide some general data here, but remember that different studies and different measures yield different data, and it is most important to know the data of the particular institution you are serving. How are students hurting?

- Nearly half of all college students report struggling with anxiety, and at least 40 percent report debilitating depression. Half have made use of counseling services, and roughly a quarter have taken psychotropic medications in the past year (Novotney, 2014).
- Sixty percent of college students drank alcohol in the past month, with two-thirds of those students engaging in binge drinking (National Institute of Alcohol Abuse and Alcoholism, 2015).
- Marijuana use on campus has tripled in the past two decades, and recent legalization will bring difficult challenges. Abuse of Adderall, Ritalin, and MDMA (i.e., Ecstasy or Molly) is widespread, and cocaine and heroin use are on the rise.
- Five percent of men and 23 percent of women experience rape or sexual assault during the undergraduate years (Rape, Abuse & Incest National Network, 2015).
- Female students, international students, LGBT students, racially minoritzed students, and other minority students report painful incidents of harassment and exclusion.
- Nearly every student at some point during college feels the pain of a broken relationship, or they have been sidelined by injury or sickness.

Pastoral care is an essential aspect of collegiate ministry. If this care is missing, many students will suffer alone, and the scope of our outreach will be thin. Pastoral love announces the hope and healing of the gospel, and it helps hurting students develop practices that will nourish lasting Christian faithfulness. Love embraces suffering, and in pastoral care, new channels for grace and compassion begin to flow.

The first thing we need to do is to preach and teach regularly about compassion, care, and suffering. Not only will those people who are suffering benefit immediately from the message, they will also be better prepared for good care when it comes. Students and colleagues who are not then suffering may also become more concerned, and a few may even join the ranks of those people who care. Beyond proclamation, we also need to model ongoing prayer on behalf of those in need—in worship services, staff meetings, and other venues where opportunities arise.

Connected to proclamation is symbolic leadership. When Christian leaders embody the love of God as well as Christian virtues like compassion, and when they do so not as a show but as a sign, they live a cruciform life and reveal radiant hope. Symbolic leadership happens through hospital visitation, attending to the marginalized and demoralized (the widows and orphans of our world), and the inked ministry of 1000 cards. I was never much of a card man—until I recently broke my neck in a terrible mountain biking accident. Recovery was rugged, and initially, due to pain and frustration, I could not formulate a sentence of prayer. Then every day at 4:00 P.M., the mailman came with an armload of cards from family, friends, campus colleagues, and my caring church. As a result, I was reminded that the body of Christ is beautiful and that I want to be like these people—and my spirit began to heal along with my body.

Campus ministers and those people serving in residence life need to be actively available. Common practice among faculty is to post office hours when students seeking help or advice can track them down. We need to offer this availability more and more. Some students will come to our offices seeking pastoral guidance, but students who are hurting may need us to take first steps toward them. If we know international students are lonely, LGBT students feel unwelcome, or some group has experienced crisis of one sort or another, we should step toward those students to display concern and availability.

On most campuses, there is way more hurt than there is help. Chaplains and counselors are often overwhelmed by need, and many are consumed by it. The courage to step out in care needs to be balanced by the skill of setting boundaries. Depending upon the campus, the duties of the ministry office, and the composition of the staff, different strategies will be developed for responding to cases that require intensive care—those cases that require ongoing counseling or need to be triaged before being handed off to professionals better equipped for the physical or emotional need. Of course, chaplains should remain involved in the cases that require a pastor's expertise—particularly those cases that involve a crisis of faith or identity—but some situations are rightly passed on to the care of others. Roughly a quarter of a chaplain's time or of the staff's time should be dedicated to pastoral care, but not too much more than that. The witness of the office—and the gospel—takes place not simply through pastoral care but in other works of teaching, training, missions, worship, and service, to name a few.

Because student need is nearly endless, and the time of every chaplain, educator, and student affairs professional is limited, we need to creatively engage in the administration of love. Caring colleagues and student leaders need to be recruited and trained to serve in a diaconal capacity. A network of care moves hope one step closer to those students in need. Members of the care network can be trained to comfort and support suffering students. Colleagues in the student affairs division often function as a care network, and with strategic effort and training, the network can be stretched across departments and into residence halls. A care network is a good strategy for expanding the reach of love, and if done well, it can be an investment for Christian growth in the caregivers. If the network of care grows in depth and reach, then this growth is a huge step toward developing a caring culture and community.

Christian leaders on campus must value the vulnerable, and we must be willing to be vulnerable. "But we have this treasure in jars of clay to show that this all-surpassing power is from God and not from us" (2 Cor. 4:7). Love calls us to the suffering and to suffer. In such ministry, the radiance of God may beam through us.

Soul Care

Care of souls—I love and I loathe this phrase. I love it because it has a rich history, and it envisions a calling that is tender and deep. I loathe it because, in a culture steeped in body-soul and sacred-secular dualisms, it suggests that the concerns of ministry are "merely spiritual" and not profoundly embodied, social, and intellectual. A holistic Hebrew notion of soul is worth recovering, and it follows the Hebrew notion of the heart. The heart is not merely a blood-pumping organ or the fount of feelings; it is the core of human allegiance and action. "Guard your heart, for everything you do flows from it" (Prov. 4:23). Soul is not some disembodied component of the person; soul *is* the person, and it focuses on the dimension of each one of us that is beautifully complex, inescapably relational, and inescapably related to God.

My reservation regarding "care of souls" also applies to this more commonly used notion: "spiritual formation." Some recognize the wide range of social and reflective practices involved in spiritual formation, but once again, where dualism reigns, it is easy to forge a strategy of spiritual formation that is an individualistic pursuit of soul bliss and not the communal pursuit of kingdom faithfulness that is the true end of Christian formation. I have tried to revive practices of discipleship as well as the use of the word itself. Dunn and Sundene (2012) provided strong arguments for discipleship throughout *Shaping the Journey of Emerging Adults*. Perhaps this is unnecessarily "old school." I have one colleague who thinks that discipleship is stained with patriarchal connotations, since the twelve disciples were all men. Others think the first-century methods of the Master are largely irrelevant for our modern day. I, however, see much more than a method in the model of Jesus's discipleship. He operates from a profound understanding of the human person and human transformation as he engages the disciples in relational ministry and experiential challenges. His teaching is persistently about the kingdom, and Jesus continuously keeps this key outcome in view: forging faithful followers.

All of that said, the generic notion of spiritual formation does provide common ground for Christians to unite with other curious religionists and humanists in exploring student patterns of integrating belief and life. And I do not mean to disparage the wonderful bounty of resources that are available for the pursuit of Christian spiritual formation. (A short list of resources is provided at the end of the chapter.) These authors have contributed immensely to Christian renewal and life-shaping practices. In the spirit of these books of disciplines, I will list seven disciplines, even though this list is far from complete. Think of these seven suggestions as kingdom streets, all leading toward the throne of the reigning king. Those people engaged in Christian ministry can strategize about ways to pave these streets in their own academic communities:

- Knowing and enjoying the gospel—that it offers forgiveness, reconciles relationships, and leads ultimately to the restoration of all things. Stroll this lovely avenue every day.
- Following the teachings and calls of the Lord Jesus, leading to fellowship with Father, Son, and Holy Spirit, and to a life of spirited mission in God's world. This street will be a rugged way at times.
- Devouring the Word by regular and prayerful reading of the Scriptures, studying and memorizing the Scriptures, and listening to the Word preached in the context of church and worship. Take this road with others.
- Communicating with God on the quiet path of prayer with faith, honesty, humility, boldness, and persistence.
- Serving the church and community by developing relationships, seeking reconciliation, providing leadership, pursuing justice, and investing in others.
- Celebrating with others and sacrificing for their well-being.
- Seeking to see the entire creation as the Lord's and to imagine all of life and culture as faithful testimony to the Lord's goodness, provision, and reign.

In other words, the fundamentals of soul care are kerygmatic, Christocentric, biblical, relational, other-directed, communal, and life-embracing. This journey is one for a lifetime. The streets lead to the throne and, from the throne, to every nook and corner of the kingdom.

Not only should chaplains preach and teach about these core dimensions of the Christian life, we must model them as well. Students sniff out hypocrisy a mile away, so our own pursuit of the nearness of the Lord must be genuine. Most of the time, however, students will not be inspired by us. God's Spirit is at work elsewhere and through others, and our job is to get students connected to that elsewhere. Much of the caring work of campus ministry is connecting students to other mentors so they can witness mature faith in action. Students benefit immensely by engaging in activities such as working at a Christian summer camp; helping to lead a youth program or weekly worship at a local congregation; joining a campus Bible study; or participating with some group committed to social justice, environmental stewardship, or food distribution. We need to connect students to already existing programs that will nurture them, and if these are missing, we need to do the work of developing groups, programs, and mentors.

Few Christians use the phrase *care of souls*, but most are perfectly comfortable with the label *spiritual formation*. I would rather call it *transformational discipleship*—because that says something about the goal (no longer conformed but transformed, as in Rom. 12:1–2) and the means (slow, relational nurture). I also like to talk about *multifaceted faithfulness*, and that phrase has not exactly caught on either. The final section explores this idea.

Student Cares

While there are many calls, some are completely insignificant. This culture (and every culture) is full of voices, each beckoning for those people who will listen to buy, believe, go, or do something. Students, like the rest of us, often listen to the wrong calls and come to care about the wrong things. In biblical context, we encounter religious impostors, idols that call the people of God away from faithfulness. The ministry of the prophets was primarily reminding Israel of her covenant callings and decrying the cacophony of calls from impostor gods and selfish leaders. In similar fashion, prophetic ministry invites students to respond to the calls of the Lord that lead to life and to resist the culture's calls that lead to destruction.

Discerning the true *vox deus* and the true calls of the Lord is the life-long work of engaging the Scriptures and reflecting on the character and purposes of God. We must help students move beyond the fixation of employment. While students do have important work to do in assessing their gifts and passions and exploring opportunities for service and livelihood, this one call often becomes the earworm—the tune that plays over and over in their minds like an advertising ditty. I am convinced this call is discerned much more clearly when we are attentive to the symphony of divine calls inviting us into a fuller life of faithfulness. An illustration in the first person may help to clarify this:

- I am not *merely* a chaplain. That is not the most central or delightful or rewarding call of my life.
- I am a child of the living God, reconciled to the Father by the Son, being renewed by the Holy Spirit. The call to enjoy this fellowship is deep, delightful, life-ordering, and life-giving.
- I am a son to my parents. My parents were not Christians, but they were exceptionally loving. My mom still is, and my father has passed away. I am called to honor them both, and even if they were not good parents, I would have to figure out what it means to honor them all my life long.
- I am a husband to my wife. I was not born married to sweet Christine, but that was a commitment we made, and now my life is defined by this calling—being a loving and faithful husband to my wife.
- I am a stepdad to my stepdaughters. There is not a chapter in the Bible on this, but loving my girls means caring for them as my very own.
- I am a friend, and by God's grace, I have a few friends. My life is made all the richer through them, and I honor God by the ways I encourage, enjoy, and pray for them.
- I am a steward. In Genesis, we learn that human beings were created in the image of God and that one of our primary duties is to steward the creation. And since everything belongs to the Lord, I steward all I have—my money, home, time, and few talents. Living according to these calls to stewardship saves me from various obsessions and fears.
- I am a neighbor. We have lived in neighborhoods where this calling was a difficult one, but right now we live on a street that is crowded with lovely neighbors, and caring for them seems natural. Jesus reminds us that this call is always a stretching one because enemies, strangers, and outcasts are also my neighbors.

- I am a teaching elder. We are all called to be the church and not to forsake gathering together. How we serve the body and what commitments we make will depend on many things. My training and commitment shape my ecclesial calling, and yours will too.
- I am a grateful aesthete. God has given us a world full of tastes, colors, textures, sounds, and jaw-dropping beauty. God has given us the capacity for enjoying food, music, poetry, and streams. While pleasures can become idols, enjoying the goodness of God and expressing gratitude is a fundamental call I am delighted to pursue.
- I am a concerned citizen. This call is an extension of the call to love my neighbor, and in this call I am also giving attention to an aspect of cultural stewardship. I am called to attend to my social-political context, care about essential institutions, pray for institutional leaders, and contribute to institutional renewal in some particular way.

These calls (and others as well) shape the cares of my life, and I enjoy caring about these things. Caring about these things leads me to a life that is meaningful, balanced, relational, and loving. While my delight, comfort, and support are ultimately found in the living Lord Jesus, I attend to these calls as an expression of my faithful love for him. Consequently, I find delight, comfort, and support in these pursuits. I will never respond perfectly and completely to any one of these calls, and it is comforting to know that I do not have to! Christ himself is my righteousness, so my pursuits are expressions of love. I will certainly be more motivated to explore some areas rather than others—accumulating more wisdom in this domain or that one—a reality that is also all part of the plan. When I am tethered together with other believers (call it the church) who have different gifts and concerns, we get to bring our loving wisdom together for the good of the order. Christian faithfulness is not an attempt to earn favor, and it should not be a lonely ordeal. It is an invitation to a lifetime of loving pursuits and shared discoveries.

In this nest of calls I find myself readied for the high calling of educational ministry. I like to think of this call not so much as my call to ministry but my ministry of calls. I preach and teach multifaceted faithfulness. I advise and counsel it. I suggest books and programs designed to pursue it. But unless students see that this faithfulness is livable and lovely, I sound like another barker at the circus calling out for attention. Discipleship takes place in relationship; it is life on life; it is slow; it has always been the path of transformation; it is the way of the kingdom.

Discerning calls is not enough; rather, students must also be prepared to respond with courage and compassion. The path is theological, but it is also about developing Christian affections—coming to love God and to love the things that God loves—and Christian character. And at some point, often in college, Christian growth is no longer advanced simply by observation, repetition, and participation. Commitments must be made and pursued with faithful diligence. Some of those commitments will be lifelong, and others will evolve or revolve. Making commitments is the central challenge of emerging adulthood, and it lies at the heart of identity formation, purpose formation, relationship formation, academic formation, and faith formation.

In a nutshell, ministry is loving the Lord with heart, soul, mind, strength, and loving your neighbor as yourself. Put another way, it is following the Lord Jesus onward and upward in kingdom service. Collegiate ministry is doing this work in an academic setting where most of the neighbors are students. Educators and student affairs professionals do this by caring for students and helping them to care about the right things, with hope and prayer that they would respond to the life-giving calls of the Lord.

Recapping:

- Caring is gracious love on the move; calling is callings, and the Lord has revealed a rich array of calls for Christian faithfulness.
- We need to know college students better and to help others know and love them too.
- We need to enter the hurt world of college students and provide hope and comfort.

- We need to invite students to participate in the gospel-anchored means of grace designed to bring life and growth.
- We need to provide a kingdom vision of life and culture and to help connect students to the One who calls them to multifaceted faithfulness.

References

Andrade, A. (2014). Using Fowler's faith development theory in student affairs practice. *College Student Affairs Leadership 1*(2), n.p. Retrieved from https://scholarworks.gvsu.edu/cgi/viewcontent.cgi?article=1014&context=csal

Arnett, J. (2004). *Emerging adulthood: The winding road from the late teens through the twenties.* New York, NY: Oxford University Press.

Astley, J., & Francis, L. (Eds.). (1992). *Christian perspectives on faith development.* Grand Rapids, MI: Eerdmans.

Dunn, R., & Sundene, J. (2012). *Shaping the journey of emerging adults: Life-giving rhythms for spiritual formation.* Downers Grove, IL: InterVarsity Press.

Dykstra, C., & Parks, S. D. (Eds.). (1986). *Faith development and Fowler.* Birmingham, AL: Religious Education Press.

Fowler, J. (1981). *Stages of faith: The psychology of human development and the quest for meaning.* New York, NY: Harper & Row.

Fowler, J. (1987). *Faith development and pastoral care.* Minneapolis, MN: Fortress Press.

Fowler, J. (2000). *Becoming adult, becoming Christian: Adult development and Christian faith.* San Francisco, CA: Jossey-Bass.

Koyama, K. (1980). *Three mile an hour God.* Maryknoll, NY: Orbis Books.

Lindholm, J., Mallorca, M., Schwartz, L., & Spinoza, H. (2011). *A guidebook of promising practices: Facilitating college students' spiritual development.* Seattle, WA: CreateSpace.

Marcia, J., Waterman, A., Matteson, D., Archer, S., & Orlosky, J. (1993). *Ego identity: A handbook for psychological research.* New York, NY: Springer Publishing.

National Institute of Alcohol Abuse and Alcoholism. (2015). *College drinking.* Retrieved from https://pubs.niaaa.nih.gov/publications/CollegeFactSheet/CollegeFactSheet.pdf

Novotney, A. (2014). Students under pressure. *Monitor on Psychology, 45*(8), 36. Retrieved from http://www.apa.org/monitor/2014/09/cover-pressure.aspx

Parker, S. (2011). Spirituality in counseling: A faith development perspective. *Journal of Counseling & Development, 89,* 112–119. doi:10.1002/j.1556-6678.2011.tb00067.x

Parks, S. D. (2000). *Big questions, worthy dreams: Mentoring young adults in their search for meaning, purpose, and faith.* San Francisco, CA: Jossey-Bass.

Placher, W. (2005). *Callings: Twenty centuries of Christian wisdom on vocation.* Grand Rapids, MI: Eerdmans.

Rape, Abuse, and Incest National Network. (2015). *Campus sexual violence: Statistics.* Retrieved from www.rainn.org

Setran, D., & Kiesling, C. (2013). *Spiritual formation in emerging adulthood: A practical theology for college and young adult ministry*. Grand Rapids, MI: Baker Academic.

Smith, C., & Denton, M. L. (2009). *Soul searching: The religious and spiritual lives of American teenagers*. Oxford, UK: Oxford University Press.

Smith, C., & Snell, P. (2009). *Souls in transition: The religious and spiritual lives of emerging adults*. Oxford, UK: Oxford University Press.

Stanard, R. P., & Painter, L. (2004). Using a faith development model in college counseling. *College Student Affairs Journal, 23*, 197–207. Retrieved from https://scholarworks.gvsu.edu/cgi/viewcontent.cgi?article =1014&context=csal

Wolfe, T. (2004). *I am Charlotte Simmons: A novel*. New York, NY: HarperCollins.

Wuthnow, R. (1998). *After heaven: Spirituality in America since the 1950s*. Oakland, CA: University of California Press.

Wuthnow, R. (2007). *After the baby boomers: How twenty- and thirty-somethings are shaping the future of American religion*. Princeton, NJ: Princeton University Press.

A Short List of Resources for Christian Spiritual Formation

Barton, R. H. (2006). *Sacred rhythms: Arranging our lives for spiritual transformation*. Downers Grove, IL: IVP Books.

Barton, R. H. (2010). *Invitation to solitude and silence: Experiencing God's transformative presence*. Downers Grove, IL: IVP Books.

Claiborne, S., Wilson-Hartgrove, J., & Okoro, E. (2010). *Common prayer: A liturgy for ordinary radicals*. Grand Rapids, MI: Zondervan.

Foster, R. (1978). *The celebration of discipline: The path to spiritual growth*. San Francisco, CA: HarperCollins.

Goggin, J., & Strobel, K. (2013). *Reading the Christian spiritual classics: A guide for Evangelicals*. Downers Grove, IL: IVP Academic.

Howard, E. (2008). *The Brazos introduction to Christian spirituality*. Grand Rapids, MI: Brazos Press.

Law, W. (1978). *A serious call to a devout and holy life*. New York, NY: Paulist Press.

Miller, P. (2009). *A praying life: Connecting with God in a distracting world*. Colorado Springs, CO: NavPress.

Nouwen, H. (2003). *The way of the heart: Connecting with God through prayer, wisdom, and silence*. New York, NY: Ballantine Books. (Original work printed 1981)

O'Connor, E. (1968). *Journey inward, journey outward*. New York, NY: Harper & Row.

Thomas, G. (2010). *Sacred pathways: Discovering your soul's path to God*. Grand Rapids, MI: Zondervan.

Thompson, M. (1995). *Soul feast: An invitation to the Christian spiritual life*. Philadelphia, PA: Westminster John Knox Press.

Whitney, D. (2014). *Spiritual disciplines for the Christian life*. Colorado Springs, CO: NavPress.

Willard, D. (1988). *The spirit of the disciplines: Understanding how God changes lives*. San Francisco, CA: HarperOne.

8

CARING ENOUGH TO MENTOR COLLEGE STUDENTS WITH DISABILITIES

ROGER D. WESSEL

Ball State University

LARRY MARKLE

Ball State University

Why should educators in higher education care about access to, and success in, higher education for students with disabilities?

Most college educators (faculty and staff) will interact with students who have some combination of disabilities. Since education is often a way for students with disabilities to level the playing field and a process to gain recognition and respect (Paul, 1999), those of us who work with these students should care for them by facilitating heightened self-determination and self-management skills (Getzel & Thoma, 2008) as well as social skills. Higher education is also a way for them to gain sound qualifications for future employment (Fuller, Healey, Bradley, & Hall, 2004), as well as other positive outcomes.

Virginia Held (2006), in her book *The Ethics of Care*, suggested caring for others is a personal decision that demonstrates pivotal moral action in our interpersonal relationships. Although she is not the first scholar to theorize about the influence of morality on our behavior (for example, Carol Gilligan [1982] and Lawrence Kohlberg [1975]), she takes a refreshingly simplistic approach by encouraging us to focus on developing caring relationships because *it is the right thing to do.*

In this chapter, we will answer the "why should we care" question by providing a legal context for expectations of care, followed by some philosophical underpinnings for care. We then shift from the philosophical to the practical by discussing how to create an ethic of care for students with disabilities in disability services offices, followed by an example from Ball State University's program of caring for students with disabilities through a mentorship model.

Legal Context of Caring for Students with Disabilities

Experts report varying percentages of college students who have at least one disability (e.g., National Council on Disability [2011] reported 19 percent; U.S. Department of Education [2013] reported 10.9 percent). The legislation guaranteeing access to higher education for these students is rooted in the civil rights movement (Madaus, 2011), specifically the push to foster equal opportunity and antidiscrimination for women and persons of color. Section 504 of the Rehabilitation Act of 1973, the first major civil rights law protecting individuals with disabilities, further opened the door to postsecondary education for students with disabilities. Borrowing from the language included in the Civil Rights Act of 1964 and the Title IX legislation of 1972, Section 504 states,

> No otherwise qualified handicapped individual in the United States shall, solely by reason of his handicap, be excluded from participation in, be denied the benefits of, or be subjected to discrimination under any program or activity receiving Federal financial assistance.

The more widely known Americans with Disabilities Act (ADA) of 1990 reinforced Section 504 and included antidiscrimination language that extends beyond the scope of institutions receiving federal funding. Colleges and universities are prohibited from discriminating against qualified students with disabilities. The 2008 amendments to the ADA broadened the scope of those covered under the ADA, as people with disabilities that are episodic in nature were included, and these amendments also lessened the documentation requirements that guided many postsecondary institutions. To be covered by the protections of the disability laws governing higher education, students must be "otherwise qualified." This statement is a very important phrase, meaning that students with disabilities must meet the same standards (i.e., admissions, academic, program, and conduct) as students without disabilities.

There is a significant legal difference when comparing how students with disabilities are supported in postsecondary institutions versus secondary education. The Individuals with Disabilities Education Act (IDEA) of 2004 is the primary law for secondary schools relative to students with disabilities. IDEA indicates it is the school's responsibility to provide specialized instruction to students with disabilities and to modify the curriculum if necessary to tailor it to the individual student's needs. IDEA's provisions do not apply to postsecondary schools.

At the postsecondary level, it is the student's responsibility to disclose the disability and provide appropriate medical or psychological documentation to support the request for accommodations. As described above, Section 504 and the ADA are the laws that lay out the responsibilities for colleges and universities regarding students with disabilities. Institutions are prohibited from discriminating against qualified students with disabilities, but there is no requirement that the curriculum be modified specifically for a student with a disability (Madaus & Shaw, 2004).

One way to describe the difference in disability services in the secondary and postsecondary venues is that K-12's goal is, if possible, to ensure the success of the students with disabilities; higher education's goal is to provide equivalent access and reasonable accommodations for the student. As mentioned above, K-12 personnel may modify standards and construct the curriculum to meet the specific needs of that student. Colleges and universities, however, ensure that the student with disabilities has access to the college's curricular and cocurricular offerings and will provide accommodations to facilitate access to its programs and academic requirements (Markle & Knight, 2013), but they do not ensure success.

The Office for Civil Rights (OCR) in the U.S. Department of Education oversees postsecondary institutions' compliance with Section 504 and the ADA. If a student with a disability feels that a college or university has discriminated against him or her, the student can file a complaint with OCR. Staff from OCR would then investigate and, if necessary, issue a letter of findings outlining steps with which the institution must comply in order to maintain compliance with federal law. Though it has not previously occurred, it is possible that, if the institution does not comply, then OCR could withhold federal funds from the institution. In addition to legal decisions determined by the court system related to higher education, letters of finding from OCR have helped colleges and universities determine best practices in serving students with disabilities and remaining compliant with federal law (Jarrow & Lissner, 2005).

Philosophical Underpinnings for Caring for Students with Disabilities

Although there are many scholars whose ideas could serve as philosophical underpinnings for our work with college students with disabilities, we often return to three higher education favorites—Arthur Chickering, Nancy Schlossberg, and Vincent Tinto—and their work related to the transition to, and what it takes to be successful in, college.

Arthur Chickering (1969) with Reisser (1993) is best known for his work on the psychosocial theory of educational identity. He identified multiple vectors as a conceptual map to help determine identity-related issues during the collegiate years. These vectors build upon each other and provide a comprehensive overview of psychosocial development. Several of the vectors (i.e., developing competence, moving through autonomy toward interdependence, developing mature interpersonal relationships, establishing identity) may be experienced differently by students with disabilities than by other subpopulations of college students. Physical and interpersonal competence may differ because the challenges of autonomy arise for this population of students when they realize that, with the advent of their collegiate careers, their personal care is now primarily their responsibility. Building and establishing relationships with others who have disabilities can also be a developmental experience, as can building relationships with students who are not disabled. And, establishing an identity, defining one's true self-path, may be different for students with disabilities. Discovering one's identity is a learning process that occurs gradually over time, with periods of success and failure (McCarthy, 2007). A large part of establishing identity for college students with disabilities is tied to building self-advocacy skills (Hadley, 2011).

Nancy Schlossberg's (1981; 1984; 1989) transition theory demonstrates that adaptation to life changes is a complex process, and adults in transition need to adjust to their new environments. She defined transition as an event, or nonevent, that results in a change in assumptions about oneself or the world. She noted that individuals must adapt to the new roles, relationships, and behaviors required by the transition. Schlossberg described three particular factors affecting an individual's transition process: characteristics of the individual, perception of the transition, and characteristics of the pre- and post-transition environments. The greater the difference in the pre- and post- environments, for instance, the more complex the transition becomes. Because college students with disabilities are engaged in a complex transition from K-12 to their new home in higher education, it is important for educators to be aware of transition theory to best help students adapt to their new settings, roles, relationships, and responsibilities.

Vincent Tinto's (1987; 1993; 2012) theory of individual departure demonstrates the difficulty many students experience when transitioning from high school to college. He used the rites of passage model created by Van Gennep (1909/1960) to suggest that college students undergo three stages of transition as they adjust to and assimilate into college life: separation, transition, and incorporation. During this transitional period, students depart from their families and high school communities and begin to make the transition to college. He also discussed the importance of students' goals, external commitments, and academic and social institutional experiences that integrate them into the collegiate experience. The absence of integration arises from a lack of institutional fit and isolation, happening when students do not fit into at least one of the multiple subgroups within the university community. Tinto indicated that disadvantaged students, including those with disabilities, are more likely to experience difficulty during the transition stage.

Because students with disabilities often encounter significant transitional issues from high school to college (e.g., only 60 percent of persons with disabilities even enroll within eight years of leaving high school [Newman et al., 2011]), Chickering, Schlossberg, and Tinto's theories have many care-related implications for college educators to consider. Students with disabilities often require reasonable academic accommodations in order to be successful. And, the greatest disadvantage may be the lack of social acceptance, as stigma related to having a disability may be the more significant transitional issue to higher education success (Trammell & Hathaway, 2007).

Disability Services: Creating an Ethic of Care on Campus

Postsecondary institutions are required to have an office or staff member responsible for facilitating accommodations for students with disabilities, and the contact information for this person or office should be easily accessible (Duncan & Ali, 2011). The common names of these offices include disability services, the disability resource center, and accessibility services. The offices are housed in various administrative units on campuses, with the majority being within the divisions of academic or student affairs. The primary responsibilities of disability services professionals are to facilitate reasonable accommodations for students with disabilities and educate the campus community on best practices in providing access and opportunity for students with disabilities (Duffy & Gugerty, 2005).

The initial programs created to care for students with disabilities on college campuses came as a result of veterans returning home after the First and Second World Wars. These programs began to include nonveterans with disabilities, and, by the early 1970s, following the success of the civil rights movements for women and minorities, students with disabilities gained greater access to higher education (Madaus, 2011). When most institutions began offering services for students with disabilities in response to Section 504 or the ADA, those services were focused on students with apparent disabilities, such as mobility or sensory impairments.

Beginning in the 1990s, more students with nonapparent disabilities began seeking services on campus. Students with learning disabilities and attention deficit disorder began disclosing these disabilities in greater numbers during this time, followed in recent years by students with psychological disabilities and autism spectrum disorders. At the authors' institution, students with nonapparent disabilities now comprise approximately 90 percent of the students who have disclosed their disabilities.

Disability services professionals work with students with disabilities who disclose their disabilities to their institution and seek accommodations. These accommodations typically include testing accommodations (commonly extended time, readers, and scribes), note-takers in classes, and textbooks in accessible formats. Disability services staff members often partner with other campus offices such as housing, parking, facilities, information technology, and others to ensure accessibility throughout their campuses.

Disability accommodations are determined on a case-by-case basis after a review of medical documentation and a discussion with the student about the important elements in establishing the appropriate accommodations. Students with the same disability diagnosis may have completely different levels of ability and thus request different accommodations. It is helpful to understand the broad categories of disabilities (listed below) represented on campuses today and the types of accommodations frequently requested (Markle & Knight, 2013).

Autism Spectrum Disorders

Many students with autism struggle socially with, and often do not pick up on, social cues that come naturally for others. Some students with autism may require the typical testing accommodations described above, and they may require more structure from faculty members than other students. Single rooms in residence halls are sometimes requested by students with autism.

Blind and Visually Impaired

Students with visual impairments benefit greatly from adaptive technology. Options include textbooks in digital formats with screen-reading software that reads aloud the text and magnification software that enlarges the text on the screen. For Braille readers, the student can access the text electronically and read the text in Braille using a handheld device that refreshes the Braille characters line by line. Common accommodations may include extended time on exams, provision of a reader and/or scribe and adaptive technology on exams, and copies of the instructor's or a peer's notes.

Chronic Health Conditions

An increasing number of students disclose conditions such as cancer, diabetes, and epilepsy. A common manifestation of the disability for students with chronic health conditions is that they may miss class time due to flare-ups of the disability. Accommodations that may be helpful for these students are flexibility with attendance policies and modified due dates.

Cognitive Disabilities

This category includes learning disabilities, attention deficit/hyperactivity disorder (ADHD), and brain injuries. This is the most prevalent category of students with disabilities on most campuses. Testing accommodations are typically what these students request. Extended time to complete exams (time-and-a-half to double the allotted time) is helpful, as it allows the student time to process and respond to the exam questions. Students with ADHD often request to take exams outside the classroom in a location with reduced distractions. Students with dyslexia and other learning disabilities may also request that exam questions be read aloud to them, either using adaptive technology or a human reader.

Deaf and Hard-of-Hearing

American Sign Language (ASL) is often the primary language for a student who is congenitally deaf. These students may request sign language interpreters for classes and meetings on campus. For students who are deaf but do not know or use ASL, a court reporter is often hired to provide a real-time transcription for the student. Other accommodations that are helpful include captioning for media and copies of the instructor's or a peer's notes.

Psychological Disabilities

The number of students disclosing mental illness on college campuses has drastically increased in recent years. These conditions include bipolar disorder, anxiety and panic disorders, depression, obsessive-compulsive disorder, and schizophrenia. As with chronic health conditions, a common manifestation of the disability is occasional class absences. If appropriate, flexibility with attendance and due dates may be requested. Testing accommodations, such as extended time and a location with reduced distractions, are often implemented for these students.

Mobility and Orthopedic Impairments

Students with mobility disabilities range from quadriplegics using wheelchairs to students with arm or hand impairments that affect typing or writing. Physical access on campus is critical for students who use wheelchairs, including residence hall rooms that are equipped with access features such as adapted bathrooms and push-button door openers. Classroom accommodations often include extended time for exams, provision of a scribe for exam questions, and copies of the instructor's or a peer's notes.

Ball State University's Mentoring Model for Students with Disabilities

Higher education research consistently indicates students who engage with faculty members are more likely to persist to graduation than students who do not (National Survey of Student Engagement, 2006). Additional research has described the struggle that students with disabilities regularly experience as they transition into college, often because the college approach to disability services may differ drastically from that of the high school. Sadly, students with disabilities often graduate from college at lower rates than those without disabilities (Newman et al., 2011).

Concerns about students with disabilities fully integrating into post-secondary education led Ball State University faculty and staff members to create a faculty mentorship program for students with disabilities in 2006. The purpose of the program is to connect new students with disabilities with a professor in the student's major (Harris, Ho, Markle, & Wessel, 2011). The professor helps the student to understand academic expectations at the university and essentially personalizes the experience for the student within the academic department. Although the mentoring is intended to last during the student's first year, some faculty members have continued mentoring their students over their time at Ball State and beyond, with some serving as references for employment and graduate school.

Ball State's Office of Disability Services invites new students with disabilities to participate in the program. Students with disabilities volunteer to be mentored by a professor, and an introductory email is sent to the student and professor to make the connection between the two. After an initial meeting between the student and faculty member, the two mutually determine how often and where they will meet for the remainder of the year. Some meet weekly or monthly the first semester, while others meet as needed or electronically. In meetings with the students, faculty members have reported they provide advice to the students on their coursework, discuss university resources, and introduce them to other faculty members within the department (Patrick & Wessel, 2013).

A recent study (Markle, Wessel, & Desmond, 2017) demonstrated the efficacy of the mentorship program for students with disabilities. The longitudinal study assessed year-two retention and graduation rates (four- and six-year rates) for students with disabilities in the program, compared with those students with disabilities who chose not to participate and students without disabilities who matriculated in the same years. Students with disabilities participating in the mentorship program outperformed students with and without disabilities in the year-two retention rate and in four- and six-year graduation rates. These data suggest that faculty engagement with students with disabilities, such as is offered through the faculty mentorship program, can play a pivotal role in providing them with the academic and social support that is critical for success in college (Tinto, 1993).

Students with disabilities are not the only population benefiting from the program. Faculty and staff participants reported a stronger understanding of how best to assist students with disabilities and the resources available on campus for them (Harris et al., 2011). Additionally, the success of the mentorship program helped Ball State University receive a three-year grant from the U.S. Department of Education's Office of Postsecondary Education to help the university enhance the program by providing additional professional development opportunities for faculty and staff to ensure best practices when working with students with disabilities.

Summary

We began this chapter with a simple question: Why should educators in higher education care about access to, and success in, higher education for college students with disabilities? We attempted to make the point that federal law expects that all students, with and without disabilities, have access to postsecondary learning opportunities and that there are multiple theoretical approaches that help us support student transition into higher education and persistence to graduation. But we also hope the motivation for faculty and staff in higher education working with students with disabilities will be because *it is the right thing to do.*

Christians recognize the inherent equality and worth of all individuals (e.g., Acts 10:34; Rom. 2:11; Gal. 3:28). The ethic of care as described in this chapter challenges faculty and staff to go above and beyond to foster environments for all students to have opportunities to reach their full potential. Since college students with disabilities often struggle as they transition to college (Newman et al., 2011), more attention is often needed to help ensure that they persist to graduation. The faculty mentorship program, as described in this chapter, is one way that Christians can display love and care toward students with disabilities. The Bible is replete with examples of meaningful mentoring relationships (e.g., Elijah and Elisha, Paul and Timothy): Christ's "mentoring" of his disciples and the words of Proverbs 9:9 should spur us to find students we can mentor.

References

Americans with Disabilities Act (ADA) of 1990, 42 U.S.C.A. §12101 *et seq.* (West 1993).

Americans with Disabilities Act Amendments Act (ADAAA) of 2008, 42 U.S.C.A. § 12201. (2008).

Chickering, A. W. (1969). *Education and identity.* San Francisco, CA: Jossey-Bass.

Chickering, A. W., & Reisser, L. (1993). *Education and identity* (2nd ed.). San Francisco, CA: Jossey-Bass.

Duffy, J. T., & Gugerty, J. (2005). The role of disability support services. In E. E. Getzel & P. Wehman (Eds.), *Going to college: Expanding opportunities for people with disabilities* (pp. 89–115). Baltimore, MD: Brookes.

Duncan, A., & Ali, R. (2011). *Students with disabilities preparing for postsecondary education: Know your rights and responsibilities.* Retrieved from the U.S. Department of Education Office for Civil Rights website: https://www2.ed.gov/about/offices/list/ocr/transition.html

Fuller, M., Healey, M., Bradley, A., & Hall, T. (2004). Barriers to learning: A systematic study of the experience of disabled students in one university. *Studies in Higher Education, 29,* 303–318. doi:10.1080/03075070410001682592

Getzel, E., & Thoma, C. (2008). Experiences of college students with disabilities and the importance of self-determination in higher education settings. *Career Development for Exceptional Individuals, 31,* 77–84. doi:10.1177/0885728808317658

Gilligan, C. (1982). *In a different voice: Psychological theory and women's development.* Cambridge, MA: Harvard University Press.

Hadley, W. (2011). College students with disabilities: A student development perspective. *New Directions for Higher Education, 154,* 77–81. doi:10.1002/he.436

Harris, J., Ho, T., Markle, L., & Wessel, R. (2011). Ball State University's faculty mentorship program: Enhancing the first year experience for students with disabilities. *About Campus, 16*(2), 27–29. doi:10.1002/1bc.20058

Held, V. (2006). *The ethics of care: Personal, political, and global.* New York, NY: Oxford University Press.

Individuals with Disabilities Education Act of 2004, 20 U.S.C.A. § 1400 *et seq.*

Jarrow, J. E., & Lissner, L. S. (2005). *From legal principle to informed practice.* Waltham, MA: Association on Higher Education and Disability.

Kohlberg, L. (1975). The cognitive-developmental approach to moral education. *Phi Delta Kappan, 56,* 670–677.

Madaus, J. W. (2011). The history of disability services in higher education. *New Directions for Higher Education, 154*, 5–15. doi:10.1002/he.429

Madaus, J. W., & Shaw, S. F. (2004). Section 504: Differences in the regulations for secondary and postsecondary education. *Intervention in School and Clinic, 40*, 81–87. doi:10.1177/10534512040400020301

Markle, L., & Knight, W. E. (2013). Supporting students with disabilities: A case study. In G. McLaughlin, R. Howard, J. McLaughlin, & W. E. Knight (Eds.), *Building bridges for student success: A sourcebook for colleges and universities* (pp. 395–402). Norman, OK: Consortium for Student Retention Data Exchange.

Markle, L., Wessel, R. D., & Desmond, J. (2017). Faculty mentorship program for students with disabilities: Academic success outcomes. *Journal of Postsecondary Education and Disability, 30*, 383–390.

McCarthy, D. (2007). Teaching self-advocacy to students with disabilities. *About Campus, 12*(5), 10–16. doi:10.1002/abc.227

National Council on Disability. (2011). *National disability policy: A progress report.* Retrieved from http://www.ncd.gov/publications/2011/04152011

National Survey of Student Engagement. (2006). *Engaged learning: Fostering success of all students.* Retrieved from http://bit.ly/2n9NekQ

Newman, L., Wagner, M., Knokey, A., Marder, C., Nagle, K., Shaver, D., & Wei, X. (2011). *The post-high school outcomes of young adults with disabilities up to 8 years after high school: A report from the National Longitudinal Transition Study-2 (NLTS2).* Washington, DC: U.S. Department of Education.

Patrick, S., & Wessel, R. D. (2013). Faculty mentorship and transition experiences of students with disabilities. *Journal of Postsecondary Education and Disability, 26*, 105–118. Retrieved from https://files.eric.ed.gov/fulltext/EJ1026835.pdf

Paul, S. (1999). Students with disabilities in post-secondary education: The perspectives of wheelchair users. *Occupational Therapy International, 6*, 90–109. doi:10.1002/oti.91

Schlossberg, N. K. (1981). A model for analyzing human adaptation to transition. *The Counseling Psychologist, 9*(2), 2–18. doi:10.1177/001100008100900202

Schlossberg, N. K. (1984). *Counseling adults in transition: Linking practice with theory.* New York, NY: Spring Publishing.

Schlossberg, N. K. (1989). *Improving higher education environments for adults: Responsive programs and services from entry to departure.* San Francisco, CA: Jossey-Bass.

Section 504 of the Rehabilitation Act of 1973, 20 U.S.C.A. § 794 *et seq.*

Tinto, V. (1987). Stages of student departure: Reflections on the longitudinal character of student leaving. *The Journal of Higher Education, 59*, 438–455. doi:10.1080/00221546.1988.11780199

Tinto, V. (1993). *Leaving college: Rethinking the causes and cures of student attrition* (2nd ed.). Chicago, IL: University of Chicago Press.

Tinto, V. (2012). *Completing college: Rethinking institutional action.* Chicago, IL: University of Chicago Press.

Trammell, J., & Hathaway, M. (2007). Help-seeking patterns in college students with disabilities. *Journal of Postsecondary Education and Disability, 20*, 5–15. Retrieved from https://files.eric.ed.gov/fulltext/EJ825757.pdf

U.S. Department of Education, National Center for Education Statistics. (2013). *Digest of education statistics 2012.* Washington, DC: Author.

Van Gennep, A. (1960). *The rites of passage* (M. Vizedon & G. Caffee, Trans.). Chicago, IL: University of Chicago Press. (Original work published 1909)

9

CHRIST-CENTERED APPROACHES TO ADDRESS SEXUAL VIOLENCE AND PORNOGRAPHY

JOHN D. FOUBERT

Union University

Having studied sexual violence for twenty-five years, pornography for ten, and having followed Jesus for thirty years, I am convinced that a major underutilized force for change in the battle to lower the prevalence of sexual violence and to dismantle the stranglehold that pornography has on our culture rests with Christians who live in fellowship with one another, look to Christ for all things, and work together to counteract the sins of sexual violence and viewing pornography. There are all too many people in our society who inflict their sinful will on the bodies of others. When sexual violence is committed by one against another or when pornography is viewed, these acts involve exerting power over others in ways that are physical, social, and spiritual.

Christian Colleges

There is perhaps no place better than the Christian college to encourage believers to care enough about themselves and others to work against sexual violence and pornography use. As believers, we are called to fight efforts to undermine the bodily integrity of those made in the image of God. If we are to really live up to this calling, we have to do better than simply not commit sexual violence and avoid viewing pornography. Although data suggest that the rate of sexual violence at Christian colleges is approximately half that at other institutions, even a comparatively low rate must be vigorously fought (American College Health Association, 2013; Vanderwoerd, 2016). In the area of pornography, four out of ten men at Christian colleges view pornography at least monthly; one in thirty-three women at such institutions views as often. These rates are lower than at other colleges; but again, any instance of sin is too much (Lastoria, Bish, & Symons, 2011, p. 46; Proven Men Ministries, 2014). With God's help, student development professionals can lead their students to do far better. Toward this pursuit, we all need to engage in the spiritual battle to decimate the influence of sexual violence and sexual exploitation within and beyond our communities.

A Calling to Love

If everyone on earth lived as God commanded, we would have no sexual violence and no pornography. Indeed, if we lived as God wanted us to, we would have no sin. Yet, our present reality—after the fall, after the first coming of Christ, and before his final return—includes all manner of sin, including the sins I write about here. If there is a simply stated antidote to the existence of sin, sexual violence, and pornography, it is this: Christian love.

We are commanded to love. To whom must we show love? Virtually everyone. A partial list is that we are to love God (Luke 10:27), our neighbor (Luke 10:27), other believers (John 13:34), and our enemies (Matt. 5:44). If we all would pray fervently for God to give us the strength to love in these ways, we could dramatically decrease the comparatively lower but still too high rate of sexual violence within Christian communities. Further, we could vastly lower the use of pornography in Christian communities, and we would make a big dent in the rate of sexual violence and pornography use in the secular world as well. Love, true love, the kind that comes from God, is a powerful weapon.

Love in a Christian community is the most powerful creative force that has ever existed. After all, it was through the love of the Trinity that the universe, in all its vast expanse, was created. Of course, it was not just God the Father who created the universe. We are reminded in Genesis 1:26 that, in the beginning when the earth and its members were formed, there was community—perfect community—between the Father, Son, and Holy Spirit. "Then God said, 'Let *us* make human beings in *our* image, in *our* likeness'" (Gen. 1:26—emphasis added). The "us" and "our" in this verse helps us know there was community among the Trinity before the world began and that the power of that unity, community, and love created virtually everything. The example of community set by the Trinity presses believers on to deeper communities with one another, partly because God wants our love to overcome evil. We must challenge one another to fight evil with love and model Christ's love to others in ways we may not have considered before so that the suffering of those hurting may be assuaged and so that unnecessary pain can be avoided entirely.

Evil and an Antidote

The topic of evil is featured prominently in these pages. It is not easy to read about things so dripping with sin as pornography and sexual violence. Sexual violence happens when a person decides that his or her motivation to violate is more important than the bodily integrity of someone made in the image of God, so much so that sexual behavior is forced upon an unwilling individual. The sin of the one who commits sexual violence is never at the invitation of, nor is it the fault of, the one sinned against. One cannot, by definition, desire something against their own will. Pornography depicts a raw, unrealistic, and deeply sinful form of sexual contact that has grown increasingly violent over the last several years (Peter & Valkenburg, 2010).

A powerful antidote to the isolating impact of sexual violence and pornography use is community. Christian philosopher and martyr Dietrich Bonhoeffer offered us a great perspective on community in his influential book *Life Together*:

> So between the death of Christ and the Last Day it is only by a gracious anticipation of the last things that Christians are privileged to live in visible fellowship with other Christians. It is by the grace of God that a congregation is permitted to gather visibly in this world to share God's Word and sacrament. Not all Christians receive this blessing. The imprisoned, the sick, the scattered lonely, the proclaimers of the Gospel in heathen lands stand alone. (Bonhoeffer, 1954, p. 19)

Bonhoeffer (1954) also reminded us, even entreated us, to reflect upon the truth that "the physical presence of other Christians is a source of incomparable joy and strength to the believer" (p. 19). Fellowship is powerful, and it is a privilege that not all get to share. It is powerful in that, in fellowship with others, we look different from the world, and we gain the courage to do what we might not otherwise do. In community, we can find the strength to do battle against the evil of sexual violence and the sin of pornography. We can find the strength to do the different thing by acting to prevent sexual violence and harassment rather than merely being passive bystanders. We can also reach out and encourage our students to do the same, within community, to walk alongside people who know the pain of being a survivor. As we reach out, perhaps the best thing we can do to help is to accept the compliment given to us from the survivor that she or he trusts us with their experience. We accept that compliment by believing, listening, and not asking a lot of questions. Though our instinct may be to fix the problem, our most helpful actions are to quietly walk alongside those who are suffering, just as Christ walks alongside us.

To avoid community is foolish, yet some people fall into the temptation of believing that they do not need community, that they only need themselves and God. Author and pastor Andy Stanley noted, "Our enemy's most successful strategy is to isolate us so he can attack and destroy us. Sheep are never attacked in herds" (Stanley & Willits, 2004, p. 31). Of course, sheep are attacked when they are separated from the flock. That is one reason why a shepherd will go to such great lengths to find that lost sheep—and why our Shepherd will work so hard to pursue us if we are lost. And it is to the flock—to the community—that we are returned. We all need the flock. In a flock, we are loved, we are fed, we avoid danger, and we recover from hurt.

Our need for the love and presence of others is not only shown to us in Scripture but also by scholars who study physical health. In a longitudinal study, scholars used very sophisticated methods to follow people's health over nine years. They found the most isolated people were three times more likely to die than those with strong relational connections. The researchers also found that people who have bad health habits but strong social ties live longer than people with great health habits but who are isolated from others (Stanley & Willits, 2004). How's that for evidence of the power of love and community?

This power of love and community can help us fight sexual sin. Sexual sin is one of many ways Satan attacks our campuses and, indeed, the Christian community at large. It is apparent that one of the most powerful weapons Satan uses to attack the church and its members is the easy availability of hard-core, violent pornography. There is no question that you have students who are struggling with this and, therefore, need your help and support. The spiritual health of the church is at stake; we need to join the prayers of the struggling to help them fight.

Today, the rate of rape has never been higher, the level of porn use never more pervasive, the violence in pornography never more severe, and human relationships never so distant, empty, and devoid of love and community (Foubert, 2017). Increasingly, almost no population is immune from the impact of pornography. Even those people who do not use pornography are affected by a culture in which its use is so commonplace. For example, those who have been exposed to large amounts of violent pornography are much less likely to step in and help a friend who is in imminent danger of being sexually assaulted (Brosi, Foubert, Bannon, & Yandell, 2011; Foubert & Bridges, 2017; Foubert, Brosi, & Bannon, 2011; Foubert & Rizzo, 2013).

A Call to Care

In this fallen world, believers in Christ are called to care. Christians are called to live differently than the world. Followers of Jesus are called to take an eternal perspective on life and not just live for the pleasure or content-ment of the moment. We are called to do the uncomfortable or even the seemingly impossible. Of course, doing his will is only impossible if we fail to call upon the source of all great actions and behaviors—the Lord. But when we do remember to call upon him, he will show his mighty strength in our weakness, and he will work through us to make the world around us take note.

In our short lives here on earth, we too often fail to stand up, step forward, and enter in to stop a situation that could result in someone else's pain. One instance in which we often fail is in stepping in to help a friend who may be in danger of sexual assault. Obviously we do not get the chance to help a friend like this frequently, but odds are, at some point, we will have the opportunity. Sadly, available data shows that there are individuals in the Christian community who abuse others, even violently, for their own selfish sexual gratification (Vanderwoerd, 2016). It would be naïve to think that there are not at least some people within Christian colleges who function as gods unto themselves and pursue sexual pleasure regardless of what the other person wants. Scripture warns us of the danger of wolves who invade the flock.

While many references to wolves refer to false prophets, the metaphor also can easily be applied to sexual violence and harassment in the church and in Christian colleges. The best data we have so far is that 2.5 percent of women on Christian college campuses experience rape or attempted rape every year (Vanderwoerd, 2016). Although this rate is lower than at other types of institutions (American College Health Association, 2013), it is unconscionable for this figure to be anything but zero.

We need to have communities in our churches and on our Christian college campuses where people feel loved enough to confess their sexual sin and all of its dangerous trappings, openly, with humility, and with the hope of experiencing true healing. A good step in this direction is to get over the fear we have of getting involved in other people's business. We can and should be the kinds of communities whose members feel loved enough to confess their sins to one another so that they might be healed (James 5:16). We can help our students to know how to appropriately and safely intervene to prevent sexual violence. Of course, I do not recommend we encourage students to jeopardize their own personal safety. We do not want them to create a situation where they are at risk of being sexually assaulted. Having made that point, there is strength in the Lord and strength in numbers of others they might call upon for assistance.

While students at Christian colleges probably have fewer opportunities than those at other schools to intervene in a drunk hook-up, they are likely to know a friend with a pornography habit who needs assertive help from a brother or sister in Christ. Our students may at some point be at a social gathering where it looks like a man is treating a woman with the lack of respect she is owed as a child of God. We all have moments when the supportive word of another can help us avoid danger.

Addressing Sin and Suffering

Despite the many efforts that Christian college educators have made to address pornography use on their campuses, we know that a good number of women and many more men on our campuses have looked at pornography at some point in the last month (Foubert, 2017). Those students who do so probably know it is wrong, but for a variety of reasons lack the strength to keep themselves from looking. Pornography is created to be enticing; it has a very strong pull on the human brain. Sadly, it also has a very strong influence, potentially leading to expectations of violence in intercourse, an inability to function sexually, and a devastating impact on the lives of people who do not always choose to be in the images viewed.

As Christians who seek to follow the command to love one another (John 13:34), we need to do a much better job walking alongside the person struggling with a past act of sexual violence, experience of sexual abuse, or a current problem with pornography. If we love one another, how do we act toward our brothers and sisters? Is it loving to intervene to help prevent sin or harm to another person? As believers, we must do a better job of holding our brothers and sisters accountable, and we must show them the compassion we are called to demonstrate. We must teach such compassion to our students. We all must be open to God's call to send us to help our brother or sister recover from or avoid sin to begin with.

Shaming others rarely results in more than an emotional shutdown. However, we can walk alongside our brother—or sister—in a Christlike fashion, reminding him of who he is in Christ, how Christ died for sin, and proclaiming to our brother that Christ lives to walk with us in victory. We know it so well it is a cliché, that God will not give us anything we cannot handle. Well, let us embrace that truth and the hope it encourages and act with the knowledge that, with God's help, we can handle any struggle or challenge. And in handling the struggle, we need to walk toward him in repentance and away from the rebellion of sin.

What does God want from us? The same thing that is experienced in the Trinity: community. The Father, Son, and Holy Spirit want relationship with us and want us to have relationship with each other akin to that found in their mysterious union. Desiring that kind of community must motivate us to fight the spiritual battles here on earth until he returns.

Caring for Students

If we act within our calling to care, one thing we will not do is say to someone, or about someone, that they deserved the sin that was done to them because of their own choices. To blame someone sinned against comes from a heart that is cold and detached from the vine of Christ. We would all do well to walk alongside, not blame, people who have been sinned against so egregiously by others.

In helping victims of sexual violence to deal with what they have experienced, it is important to understand the concept of the freeze response. Researchers have known for many years that people who experience trauma will often freeze instead of fight or flee in the face of extreme danger. A recent study from Harvard (Wilson, Lonsway, & Archambault, 2016) showed that, during a trauma, the prefrontal cortex shuts down. This part of the brain is often referred to as the thinking brain, as it is where conscious decisions are made. During trauma, brain chemicals shut it down so that we are left to habits and instincts. What happens when a threat appears, as in sexual violence, is an initial freeze, and then the body goes into fight, flight, or a second freeze. The most common response is the second freeze.

We also now know there are three types of freezing. One is a spaced-out kind of freeze called "dissociation." The second is called "tonic immobility," where the person is basically conscious but loses control over their body movements. The third is "collapsed immobility," which is much like fainting or passing out due to terror. These distinctions are important to remember, because you could hear someone say, "I just lay there. I could not move. I cannot believe I did not fight back or run away." In that case, you can explain to the person who is trusting you with their experience that these freeze responses are not under conscious control. The prefrontal cortex shuts down, and their response was determined by a prewired process in their brain. A freeze is usually an automatic response, not a choice.

Another way the call to care is relevant to all of us is that we are called to be consensual in all intimate behaviors and not just in our sexual behaviors. As we work with our students, we can encourage them to give and receive effective consent by learning how to give and receive consent for something like holding hands. It honors the image of God to ask another created in that image if it is okay to hold their hand. It is a profoundly intimate gesture to show someone that you care enough about them to ask if even a small level of bodily intimacy is okay.

Most of us have seen the pain in the eyes of women and men who have used pornography, who are addicted to it, or who have broken relationships because of it. Some of us even know this pain personally. I have seen the devastation in the eyes of a man I interviewed for my book about *How Pornography Harms* (Foubert, 2017). He went to jail after he joined a file-sharing program where pornography of underage people was shared. I have heard the pain in the voice of the woman I interviewed who lived a devastating life that only got worse when she was slowly fooled into being part of the pornography industry. Moments from suicide, God sent her a ministry leader who rescues porn actors, and now she is helping to rescue others. Though most of our students are unlikely to find themselves in these types of dramatic circumstances, there is no doubt that many of our students are being hurt by pornography. As educators, we would be wise to develop strategies for helping our students avoid the temptations of pornography in the first place, as well as strategies to help those who are already struggling with its powerful addictive control. We must be gospel-centered in our approach to helping our students, and we must be willing to make sacrifices to help them find wholeness and peace.

Love Your Neighbor

As this chapter approaches a close, I will explore the topic of loving our neighbor in the midst of a time when it is evident that sin is rampant in the world. We are, of course, called to love our neighbor as ourselves. When one examines the data on today's generation of college students, it is cause for deep concern. Today's college students are more self-centered, more narcissistic, and less empathetic than any other generation studied (Twenge, 2014). One disturbing reality about the generational trend is that narcissism is one of the strongest indicators of a man who will commit sexual violence (Mouilso & Calhoun, 2016). Furthermore, a lack of empathy is a strong indicator of someone who will not intervene to help prevent sexual violence (Diamond-Welch, Hetzel-Riggin, & Hemingway, 2016). In our ministerial callings, we must be prepared for a continued generational shift toward the rising likelihood that people will mistreat each other in numerous ways because they cannot see beyond themselves. This shift adds more urgency to our responsibility to help foster humble hearts in those students we lead. We must lead them to the foot of the cross to witness the most humble act ever completed.

I am wildly optimistic that we as Christians, who are called to care and be different from the world, can inhabit this empathy gap by allowing the power of the gospel of Jesus Christ to remove our own narcissistic tendencies. Further, we can work to alleviate this lack of empathy and presence of narcissism among those we work with. The sinful nature of our culture gives Christians an opportunity to be salt and light. Foremost, people really can know we are Christians by our love for each other; our willingness to stand up, step in, and help a brother or sister, neighbor, or even an enemy out of a precarious situation; and our ability to teach others to intervene. Indeed, as Stanley and Willits (2004) reminded us, the very credibility of the life of Christ and of his gospel message in the eyes of people outside the Christian faith rests on how we who are inside the faith act differently from others. That reality means, when presented with the opportunity to be different and make a difference, both our students and we must stand up, step in, and do something.

Rick Warren (1999) once wrote about the storms of life in a way I believe relates directly to the turmoil in which survivors of sexual abuse find themselves. He said,

> The Bible teaches that there are three kinds of storms in life: storms that we bring on ourselves (as Samson and his self-induced troubles), storms that God causes (as Jesus stilling the storm on Lake Galilee), and storms that other people cause (like Paul and Silas thrown into prison). When you are the innocent party in a crisis, that last kind of storm is especially hard to take. Storms don't play favorites; Christians have problems too. (p. 70)

In closing, we all need to be more compassionate to victims of sexual violence and Christians who struggle with the sin of pornography. We need to encourage our students to love those who fall into sin or who are victims of the sin of others. We especially need to teach them this life is not about us. It is about him and what he does through us in communities modeled on the love set before us in the Trinity.

References

American College Health Association. (2013). *National College Health Assessment*. Washington, DC: Author.

Bonhoeffer, D. (1954). *Life together*. San Francisco, CA: Harper & Row.

Brosi, M. W., Foubert, J. D., Bannon, R. S., & Yandell, G. (2011). Effects of sorority members' pornography use on bystander intervention in a sexual assault situation and rape myth acceptance. *Oracle: The Research Journal of the Association of Fraternity/Sorority Advisers, 6*(2), 26–35. Retrieved from http://bit.ly/2mYPQ50

Diamond-Welch, B. K., Hetzel-Riggin, M. D., & Hemingway, J. A. (2016). The willingness of college students to intervene in sexual assault situations: Attitude and behavior differences by gender, race, age, and community of origin. *Violence and Gender, 3*(1), 49–54. doi:10.1089/vio.2015.0023

Foubert, J. D. (2017). *How pornography harms: What teens, young adults, parents, and pastors need to know*. Bloomington, IN: LifeRich Publishing.

Foubert, J. D., & Bridges, A. J. (2017). Predicting bystander efficacy and willingness to intervene in college men and women: The role of exposure to varying levels of violence in pornography. *Violence Against Women, 23*, 692–706. doi:10.1177/1077801216648793

Foubert, J. D., Brosi, M. W., & Bannon, R. S. (2011). Pornography viewing among fraternity men: Effects on bystander intervention, rape myth acceptance and behavioral intent to commit sexual assault. *Journal of Sex Addiction and Compulsivity, 18*, 212–231. doi:10.1080/10720162.2011.625552

Foubert, J. D., & Rizzo, A. (2013). Integrating religiosity and pornography use into the prediction of bystander efficacy and willingness to prevent sexual assault. *Journal of Psychology and Theology, 41*, 242–251. Retrieved from http://bit.ly/2mXOCa5

Lastoria, M. D., Bish, G. T., & Symons, C. S. (2011). Sexual behaviors. In M. D. Lastoria (Ed.), *Sexuality, religiosity, behaviors, and attitudes: A look at religiosity, sexual attitudes, and sexual behaviors of Christian college students* (pp. 30-35). Houghton, NY: ACSD.

Mouilso, E. R., & Calhoun, K. S. (2016). Personality and perpetration: Narcissism among college sexual assault perpetrators. *Violence Against Women, 22*, 1228–1242. doi:10.1177/1077801215622575

Peter, J., & Valkenburg, P. M. (2010). Adolescents' use of sexually explicit Internet material and sexual uncertainty: The role of involvement and gender. *Communication Monographs, 77*, 357–375. doi:10.1080/03637751.2010.498791

Proven Men Ministries. (2014). Pornography addiction survey (conducted by Barna Group). Retrieved from http://www.provenmen.org/2014pornsurvey/.

Stanley, A., & Willits, B. (2004). *Creating community: Five keys to building small group culture.* Colorado Springs, CO: Multnomah.

Twenge, J. M. (2014). *Generation me: Why today's young Americans are more confident, assertive, entitled and more miserable than ever before.* New York, NY: Simon & Schuster.

Vanderwoerd, J. R. (2016, March). *Sexual violence on campus: Lessons from individual and contextual factors.* Presented at the 13th Hawaii International Summit Institute on Violence, Abuse, and Trauma, Honolulu, HI.

Warren, R. (1999). *Answers to life's difficult questions: Sound advice from the Bible on our challenges, struggles, and fears.* Lincolnwood, IL: Encouraging Word.

Wilson, C., Lonsway, K. A., & Archambault, J. (2016). *Understanding the neurobiology of trauma and implications for interviewing victims.* Colville, WA: Ending Violence Against Women International. Retrieved from http://bit.ly/2ivkjq3

10

HIGHER EDUCATION AS AN EXEMPLAR OF CARE

Creating a Campus Culture of Care

TIMOTHY W. HERRMANN

Taylor University

As Christ-followers, we understand that we are called to care for others. Whether or not this calling is part of the daily work we get paid to do, we know it is a vital part of the vocation of all believers. We are heartened and hastened by 2 Corinthians 1:3–4:

> Praise be to the God and Father of our Lord Jesus Christ, the Father of compassion and the God of all comfort, who comforts us in all our troubles, so that we can comfort those in any trouble with the comfort we ourselves receive from God.

Jesus leaves no questions about the standard or centrality of care for his followers when he instructs in Matthew: "So in everything, do to others what you would have them do to you, for this sums up the Law and the Prophets" (7:12). We could review countless other scriptures to reinforce this message, but the point is so self-evident that to do so here would be of little additional benefit.

That we are called to be concerned for our brothers and sisters, care for the other, and especially care for the most vulnerable need not be argued here. It is one of the clearest themes in Scripture, and it is among the most recognizable aspects of Jesus's earthly ministry. In fact, care is so central that to call it an "aspect" is misleading; it is a purpose, a method, and a manner more than it is simply a component. It can be reasonably argued that it was the medium through which Christ illustrated who he was and who we are to him.

If this calling is so self-evident, why are so many college students, even Christian college students, hurting? Perhaps more to the point, why do so many of our hurting students feel so alone—even uncared for—during this period that is often characterized to them as the best four years of their lives? Why do so many students feel ill-equipped to cope with life's daily demands, to approach the future with confidence, or to sustain a sense of purpose that brings meaning to their struggles and challenges?

There is no simple or single answer to this question. In fact, modern American life is a cauldron of conditions that comprise a perfect storm that is increasingly assaulting the confidence, health, development, and well-being of college students. Among the most obvious factors are the breakdown of the nuclear and extended family; loss of community and shared communal values; racial tensions; societal violence; changing sexual norms and understandings of sexual identity; political vitriol; economic uncertainty; snowballing rates of illegal and prescription drug abuse; and technological change that demands rapid and repeated readjustment and that, despite its promise of connecting people, has had an isolating effect on many. While these realities are relatively apparent, there are many others that, though more subtle, also impact students' sense of well-being. For instance, concerns about the environment, ever-present and ever-escalating international tensions and humanitarian crises, and even the modern complexity of simply deciding what they should do with their lives creates a milieu of apprehensiveness that weighs heavily on emerging adults.

Though we might dispute the relative importance of any of the items in this litany of troubles, the truth that college students are troubled is indisputable. According to data from the 2016 Higher Education Research Institute (HERI) Freshman Survey, 40.8 percent of all freshmen have felt frequently or occasionally "overwhelmed by all [they] had to do." The 2015 HERI Freshman Survey indicated that 25.4 percent of students from all reporting baccalaureate institutions had parents who were either divorced or living apart, and another 3.4 percent had at least one parent who was deceased. A recent piece in *The Chronicle of Higher Education* (Zimmerman, 2017) suggested that "nearly two-thirds of college students have reported experiencing 'overwhelming anxiety' during the past year," "almost one-third reported feeling so depressed that they had trouble functioning," and almost "half said that they had felt that things were hopeless" (p. A52). Results from the 2012 annual survey of the Association for University and College Counseling Center Directors indicated that "21 [percent] of counseling center students present with severe mental health concerns, while another 40 [percent] present with mild mental health concerns" (Mistler, Reetz, Krylowicz, & Barr, 2012, p. 5).

The idea that the college years constitute a vulnerable period of life is not a recent recognition. Many years ago, esteemed higher education scholars like Sharon Daloz Parks (1986) and Alexander Astin (1977) characterized the four years of college as "critical." Such language was not intended to simply convey importance or opportunity but rather, in the developmental-psychological sense, that this period of optimal developmental opportunity is presented and must be seized for the good of the individual and society at large. In the same way that early childhood is known to be a critical period for the optimal development of language, early adulthood is a critical period for the development of meaning, purpose, faith, and commitment—the process Steven Garber (2007) has so artfully written of as "weaving together belief and behavior." The significance of the concept of critical periods that must be fully grasped is that these are not just periods of rapid growth but rather that, if humans are not nurtured and not exposed to appropriate developmental stimulation during these times, it isn't likely that optimal or potential development will occur. Thus, just as a child who is isolated from sound, conversation, and social interaction during critical periods of language development will never develop appropriate language capabilities, young adults deprived of proper care, challenge, and support will never realize a full sense of purpose or develop the necessary means for accomplishing that purpose (calling). Such a loss is not simply a loss to the student or those people close to them; rather, it is a loss to their communities, the world, and ultimately, the kingdom of God.

The chapters that comprise this monograph have examined care for college students in a variety of areas and from a variety of perspectives. Chapter authors have helped us to envision what care for students looks like in several different realms, and they have challenged us to consider how we might best think about a biblical perspective of holistic care for college students. While no such simplistic formula was employed to guide what was requested from or what was written by the contributing authors, I do hope that what has been said will help us to think more fully and more faithfully about "what Jesus would do" were he to fill one of our roles or even lead one of our institutions.

The purpose of this chapter then is to consider briefly what it means to be an institution that cares well for its students—that provides the structures and support necessary to nurture students from diverse backgrounds and with diverse needs toward wholeness and toward the fulfillment of the purposes to which they are called.

If We Want to Care Well for College Students, It Matters How We Think about Higher Education

The realities of the world in which we live render complete agreement upon the purposes of higher education impossible. And, of course, it is reasonable that different sectors of higher education and different types of institutions have different goals and purposes. However, there is a troubling development that cuts across sectors and has incredible implications for our ability to create nurturing environments for our students or to promote the ideal of an ethic of care as a mark of an educated person. In short, this development is the increasing tendency to view and educate students as "means" rather than "ends." We are guilty of treating students as revenue streams, fuel for the economic engine, laborers in accomplishing our scholarly agendas, or even as soldiers in whatever "battle of the day" we find most compelling.

Though no institution highlights this self-serving focus in its admissions materials, institutional actions and priorities often betray such an emphasis. Devoting more institutional energy to creating new revenue streams than to developing more life-giving pedagogies or more meaningful curricula speaks volumes about our real values. If our institutional values are misplaced, then we impair our students' ability to embrace proper priorities—a foundation stone of a caring community. Though Marshall McLuhan's pronouncement that "the medium is the message" has become an unchallenged truism, in recent years much of higher education is guilty of giving this maxim scant credence in the design of our programs, priorities, and spending patterns.

In recent years, the educational community and its stakeholders have made a dramatic shift toward the adoption of a utilitarian conception of higher education: one that assumes its purpose is primarily material or economic. This shift is not just a semantic exercise; it holds incredible consequences for both our students and our world. If a college education is intended to teach us how to think and how to live, then to be meaningful it must develop our intellectual faculties as well as our abilities to understand and appreciate what has value. Truly caring for our students requires us to nurture in them care for what truly matters. While this need has relevance for all segments of higher education, it is ground zero for Christ-centered institutions and Christ-imitating educators. A critical organizing theme or question in such institutions and for such educators must be, "What are we showing our students about what matters?" By nurturing the foundational notions of justice and care and responsibility in our students, we will empower and even compel them to cultivate skills and dispositions that will enable them to flourish and to be part of the creation of more just, more prosperous, and more caring communities—both on our campuses and beyond. More than twenty years ago, Neil Postman (1996) spoke to the great hope of education when he declared,

> Something can be done in school that will alter the lenses
> through which one sees the world; which is to say, that nontriv-
> ial schooling can provide a point of view from which what *is* can
> be seen clearly, what *was* as a living present, and what *will be* as
> filled with possibility. What this means is that at its best, school-
> ing can be about how to make a life, which is quite different
> from how to make a living. (p. x)

Though Christian colleges by nature exist to help students understand what constitutes "the good life" and to know what it means to live well, we are increasingly guilty of incorporating ends and means that are inconsistent with our ultimate purposes and, more to the point of this monograph, do not foster the ultimate well-being of our students. Though most of our institutional mission statements give attention to these deep and abiding values, the increasingly troubled waters of higher education have led many of our institutions to act as if their mission is simply to survive. If our ambition is to nurture student well-being, then this desire must be reflected in the way we conceive higher education—and not just how we conceive it, but how those conceptions are translated into action. Institutional practices and priorities are a far better indicator of our beliefs about education than mission or philosophy statements.

This monograph, while trying to address certain specifics about student care, is also about understanding that care is as much about "who we are" institutionally as it is about "what we do." Additionally, it is written with the recognition that caring is not primarily about services offered but rather about the way the educational experience is conceived and delivered. Thus, to care for students is to educate them well, to help them develop a strong sense of calling, to help them wrestle honestly with the big questions of life, to help them develop strong social skills and connections, to help them gain self-awareness, to help them develop and embrace a worldview that will guide them through the storms of life, to help them develop self-discipline, and to help them grow in Christlikeness. To be a caring institution, we must attend to all these things and, of course, much more. Caring institutions are committed to helping their students—through both nurture and challenge—to become their best selves.

Caring for Students Is an Institution-Wide Endeavor

Caring well for students requires an institution-wide effort; evidence of the commitment must permeate all aspects of a student's experience. While some elements of such a commitment may be programmatic and accompanied by clear strategies and tactics, being a caring institution is much deeper than these components. To be a caring college or university means that care must be embedded in the institutional ethos in a way that manifests itself throughout the campus community.

Healthcare and mental health enterprises often define the legal principle of "a duty to care" as something like the "obligation to avoid acts or omissions, which could be reasonably foreseen to injure or harm other people" (Australian Government, 2004, p. 76). Though this legal definition is helpful and represents an honorable level of client service, it stops short of the Christian ideal of loving our neighbors in a manner that makes their well-being our priority. Though this "neighbor principle" is an element of basic Christian discipleship, it seems clear the responsibility is even greater for those who aspire to educate. James 3:1 should be a sobering admonition to all who endeavor to teach: "Not many of you should become teachers, my fellow believers, because you know that we who teach will be judged more strictly." While this scripture is specifically referring to teachers of the faith, one would be hard pressed to make a clear separation between this passage and the work of educators who aspire to engage in "whole-person education" and especially those who do so within the Christian academy. Care for students is often individualized, but this care is most impactful when it is consistent with the communal environment. If we think of care for students only in terms of our own work with them, we forfeit a powerful advantage in our efforts to help them learn and grow. Hamrick, Evans, and Schuh (2002) echoed many others in noting "one of the essential factors influencing learning and the eventual outcomes of a student's learning experience is the campus environment" (p. 81). We will best care for our students and best develop in them the ambition and capacity to care for others if our campuses constitute communities of care.

Pursuing such priorities is not without cost in terms of effort, finance, or risk. This pursuit requires institutions to know and articulate who they are with the understanding that some will be attracted to this vision and some will not. This expectation is no small risk for institutions feeling the need to be all things to all people in order to compete in the ever-intensifying student recruitment race. Conversely, those institutions unwilling or unable to provide this clarity for both internal and external constituents may, in truth, not have much to offer. The first element in being an institution that cares well for students is for it to be honest about its identity so prospective students and their parents can choose wisely where they will study. Helping these students to understand and choose knowledgeably, even if that means attending another institution, is itself an act of care. Institutional fit or alignment is a prerequisite to a student feeling cared for, and institutional integrity and transparency are required for students to be capable of making this determination.

The sorts of institutions that care best for their students are those that nurture care at every organizational level. In such institutions, students will experience care, often expressed as consistent kindness, respect, consideration, thoughtfulness, integrity, and competent practice as they interact with the registrar's office, financial aid, maintenance, and dining services, as well as academic faculty, student development educators, and other administrators. Institutions that care, for example, understand and value the idea that a maintenance employee tending a campus garden is performing an act of care by creating an environment that acknowledges that souls are strengthened, blessed, and quieted by beauty. And if one of higher education's most noble purposes is to facilitate the search for the true, the good, and the beautiful, perhaps such an act is not just an enhancement to the learning environment but a central component. Willimon (1997) spoke wonderfully to the impact of the physical environment on students' education when he offered,

> Jefferson worried more about the physical setting of his
> University of Virginia (UVA) than about the curriculum. He
> designed the institution to encourage the classical ideals of con-
> versation and interaction between and among faculty and stu-
> dents, and for the observation of the old by the young. (p. 75)

The colleges and universities that care best for their students understand that programs, policies, and personnel, as well as implicit and explicit institutional values, all impact the well-being of their students.

A Caring Community Is Not a Therapeutic Community

First, let it be clear that neither this heading nor this section are intended to disparage students who have or will engage in psychological or psychiatric processes, nor our colleagues whose roles are directly connected to providing therapeutic care to students. These processes and these people are gifts to us and essential elements of colleges that care well for their students. It is not an overstatement to say that, during my days as a student development practitioner, I literally could not have done my work without the efforts, insights, and skill of these valued associates. It would be equally true to say that I have seen countless students whose lives have been enriched and, in some cases, literally saved by the work of skilled therapists. My own life and work have been strongly informed and enhanced by an academic degree in counseling. However, all these points acknowledged, a college campus is not a therapeutic community.

The term therapeutic community generally refers to holistically oriented residential treatment programs often focused on addressing substance abuse issues, but also sometimes concentrating on other sorts of mental health needs. While students may receive support in confronting serious issues and while many of our campuses do, indeed, provide wonderfully supportive environments in which to work through difficult life and mental health challenges, this therapeutic support is not fundamentally the purpose for which our colleges and universities exist. Although admittedly higher education has multiple purposes, it exists first to promote structured student learning. Even though most colleges have rightfully expanded the boundaries of the definition of student learning, without some borders, our efforts become dangerously dissipated. Stanley Fish (2004), in his often curmudgeonly but always insightful way, warned, "Don't confuse your academic obligations with the obligation to save the world; that's not your job as an academic" (para. 1).

Though Fish was speaking specifically of politicizing academic work rather than conflating education and therapy, his point has merit for this discussion. We rightly want to maximize the benefits and realize the fullest potential that education offers, but if we do not give careful attention to our primary purposes, we risk accomplishing less, not more. In order to practice the type of care that colleges and universities exist to offer, students must possess a level of emotional health and stability that allows them to meet the demands inherent in the educational process. Colleges and universities, especially small ones, do not have the resources available to provide intensive, long-term mental health support, and though the effort to do so is generally well-intentioned, it often works against the struggling student and compromises the comprehensive efforts of higher learning communities. On residential, community-focused campuses, students dealing with serious mental health concerns may not only compromise their own academic success but also the success of other students around them. Those people with a duty to care must protect the learning environment for all students. Often, a struggling student is best served both academically and in terms of their overall well-being by being encouraged to take time away from school to focus on their welfare—without having their attention divided between their mental health needs and the myriad academic and social demands that come with being a student.

While it is impossible to provide rules to determine how and when such decisions should be made, students who cannot devote appropriate attention to their academic responsibilities or who significantly detract from the learning environment around them should not be enrolled in higher education. Though given modern sensitivities, this point may seem harsh, it is, in reality, a kindness. Leaders who fail to address such situations do so to the detriment of the student and the community, and in this way, they fail to provide appropriate care. As educators, our chief responsibilities include being designers, caretakers, and guardians of the learning milieu. One of the most daunting and sobering elements of that obligation is discerning who is fit to study.

What Does It Mean to Care for College Students?

If the preceding sections of this chapter have been intended to provide a foundation or background, this segment is intended as a conversation aimed at helping educational leaders (meaning all who read these pages) to consider how to best create or facilitate the conditions necessary to promote an environment of caring on their campuses. As noted earlier, we can do great good by being caring individuals, but there is much greater power in being part of a caring community.

It is true that, on a caring campus, departments, policies, and personnel must reflect this aspiration; however, it is also true that, for better or worse, much of a student's education is provided not by the institution but by their peers. This reality represents an incredibly powerful educational concept that, quite surprisingly, receives little attention. Winston (1997) coined the term "customer input technology" to characterize the idea that "students help educate students," and he went on to note that "these . . . 'peer effects' . . . show up regularly in empirical studies of college quality—and they're certainly apparent to those of us who teach" (p. 35). I am, of course, not suggesting we only admit "caring students" but rather that all strategies to accomplish this end must consider how to best nurture students to be thoughtful, reflective, and considerate community members. Additionally, we must work to empower them educationally, emotionally, and spiritually to work toward the building of a more caring campus community. This initiative must be an active one that is addressed through a broad array of programs and practices such as chapel, residence life programming and priorities, student leadership development, and even student conduct codes and processes. While this list is not exhaustive, hopefully it prompts you to consider the places and programs on your own campus that may provide venues to address this important and life-giving priority. If we are to create genuinely caring campuses, we must understand that we are not only teaching our students to be caring themselves but that they should be challenging and encouraging their peers to do the same.

Perhaps no one has been a more effective advocate for the power and the promise of mentoring and mentoring communities than Sharon Daloz Parks. One might argue that one of the clearest connections between the ancient and the modern academy is the continued presence of the mentoring ideal. Thus, as Dr. Daloz Parks has articulated these ideas, what we have heard has resonated with us, because we understood how central they were to the heart of education and to being the kinds of educators we aspire to be. Because education is a relational endeavor, relationships are essential to being a caring community. These relationships are best facilitated by the mentoring ideal. By using the phrase "mentoring ideal," I am not specifically advocating traditional mentoring—though that is a powerful tool. Rather, I am advocating a type of college community that prizes the longstanding idea that education is best understood as the process of the older and more seasoned guides relationally passing on their experience, knowledge, and wisdom to those who are younger and less experienced. Though in many ways modern higher education has not attended well to this ideal, its appeal is still very strong. As I was writing these very words, I received my January 19, 2018, issue of *The Chronicle of Higher Education*; it bore the rather unwieldy yet compelling front-page headline "When undergraduates have a mentor, they are twice as likely to thrive after college. But only 1 in 5 have had these relationships" (Sumiano, 2018, p. 1). We need say little more to establish the connection between mentoring (in all its varied forms) and caring! Thus, the final section suggests that the foundation of a caring campus community rests on the hope of fostering the ideals of mentoring and mentoring communities.

Mentoring as a Medium for Student Care

Willimon (1997), in an article referenced earlier in this chapter, suggested that the type of environment that positively impacts the character development of emerging adults has four critical ingredients: time, place, observation, and conversation. In this brief but weighty piece, he unpacked these timeless ideas that curiously have received scant attention in our time. He argued that the development of character—broadly defined—requires that older, more experienced adults must invest meaningfully in direct interaction with students. He also suggested, as noted earlier, that colleges and universities must carefully design their spaces to maximize human encounter and encourage interaction between community members. Finally, Willimon advocated that such communities must provide routine opportunity—structured and otherwise—to allow for the observation of the older and more experienced community members by those members who are younger and less experienced. In reality, his time, place, observation, and conversation model ends up suggesting a sort of apprenticeship for life and represents a rather classical understanding of higher education.

In *The Fabric of Faithfulness*, Steven Garber (2007) observed that there are three elements present in the lives of those who successfully connect belief and behavior and whose beliefs prove resilient through the challenges of life: a worldview sufficient for the questions and crises of life; a significant mentor who incarnates this worldview; and a community that embodies the values, purposes, and convictions embedded in this worldview. Of course, Garber's thoughts resonate with those people who care for college students because the academy, especially as it is traditionally understood, addresses many of the elements necessary to facilitate this process. Furthermore, Christian educators, both in Christian higher education and in other settings, often see these components as explicit goals and purposes of the work they do.

I would suggest that Garber's (2007) and Willimon's (1997) complementary pieces provide visions or models of caring communities. Rather than explicitly addressing the programmatic and technical elements of caring for college students, they describe environments with elements that will lead to students being valued and attended to as well as environments where consideration of the big questions of life will be embedded naturally into the daily flow of things.

While these methods are not the only ways in which we will see care demonstrated in caring communities, they represent the heart of what it means to care for students. If these pieces are in place and truly attended to, many of the other necessary pieces will fall into place naturally. This point is not to suggest that such an approach should replace programmatic essentials such as counseling services. Rather, it suggests that this focus will render such services more effective as they become part of an environment that gives attention to the basic human need for caring direction and thoughtful guidance. The work of counselors and other practitioners is made more difficult when clients leave their sessions and go back into environments that are cold, unsupportive, and fail to reinforce the therapeutic process. While the care implicit in mentoring communities will not eliminate all such issues, it will certainly offer improvement.

The power of mentoring has been discussed by many individuals, and many college students express a desire to receive instruction, guidance, and advice from a trusted adviser who possesses life experience beyond their own and who demonstrates a meaningful commitment to their well-being. Colleges and universities that embrace care for students as a missional calling have great power to assist them in all of the realms that Garber (2007) and Willimon (1997) discussed.

Though many institutions would love to offer personal mentoring for all students, it is numerically impossible for most of them to do so. Nevertheless, institutions that place a high value on the mentoring ideal often look for creative ways to engage students, including the provision of peer mentoring programs, enhanced academic advising, and other initiatives intended to connect students and faculty outside of the traditional classroom. Though such programs are not a substitute for individual mentoring relationships, they may provide powerful opportunities for students to observe and connect with others whose lives offer instruction in the art of living well. Not incidentally, some of these encounters may actually provide an initiation into more formal mentoring opportunities later.

Although most institutions will be unable to offer individual mentors to all students who would benefit from them, all institutions can serve as mentoring communities. This is an immensely compelling concept that offers great promise to those who care about college students and their well-being. Parks (2011) described such communities as

> offering the gifts of recognition, support, challenge, and inspiration and incorporating certain features that distinctively honor and animate the potential of emerging adult lives. These include a network of belonging, big-enough questions, encounters with otherness, vital habits of mind, worthy dreams, and access to images (content) and practices. (p. 176)

Institutions that work to create these conditions will provide great benefit to their students and provide a model of compassionate community that these same students can replicate in the places they inhabit after graduation. Because they will have observed and experienced such places, they are far more likely to become agents of community in their homes, workplaces, churches, and neighborhoods in the future. Since community is a primary biblical value, Christian educators ought to help their students to gain greater imagination for, commitment to, and facility in promoting community in the places they dwell.

The mentoring ideal can be threatened by an over-professionalization of our work. While many professional standards are aids in caring well for students, there are some that jeopardize or disrupt the beneficial organic connection between students and educators. Thus, while appropriate professionalism and professional competency are critical elements of student care, we must also be careful not to adopt or adapt practices mindlessly without a thoughtful assessment of their appropriateness for a given setting or situation. Again, Parks (2011) offered a thoughtful reflection on this state of affairs when she suggested,

The practice and wisdom of mentoring has been weakened in our society. We compensate for this loss with a professionalism that is too often delivered without the "life-giving, caring field once provided by elders." This has contributed to fragmentation and loss of transcendent meaning for which no amount of professional expertise can compensate and has spawned assumptions that tragically widen the gap between generations. Restoring mentoring as a vital social art and a cultural force could significantly revitalize our institutions and provide the intergenerational glue to address some of our deepest and most pervasive concerns. (pp. 13–14)

This failure, while perhaps disheartening, also represents a powerful opportunity for those who believe deeply in the promise of higher education and who hope to play a part in restoring benefits that have been lost or realizing potential that remains unfulfilled. Though professional standards can be immensely beneficial in guiding practice, that benefit is compromised if our understanding and adherence to them becomes mechanical or legalistic. Former college president Milo Rediger wisely offered that "love prompts more than the law demands." While our work with students should indeed reflect alignment with professional standards and best practices, these benchmarks alone are inadequate measures of success. More importantly, our work should reflect genuine love and regard for the students we serve as well as a practical acknowledgment of what it means to be human.

Caring—Good for the Soul, but Bad for Business

In addition to working to honor mentoring and embody the values of mentoring communities, caring campuses must also approach their work with students in ways that pay tribute to their humanity and their status as image-bearers. Higher education has been so influenced by financial challenges and business modeling that our practices and priorities often appear to reflect commercial rather than educational ideals. This dynamic is not only inconsistent with the essence of a learning community, it is also inconsistent with a Christian conception of the world. Caring for our students because we believe they bear the mark of the Creator yields far different motivations, methods, and investments than those resulting from concern with their impact on the bottom line.

There are also elements of culture beyond higher education that strongly influence life within the academy. In a recent conversation, a particularly thoughtful graduate student asked me what I thought were the primary socializing forces in our culture. In responding, I suggested several of the usual suspects: the family, education, media and technology, and the church. Upon hearing my response, he said, "I think you've missed a big one—what about consumer capitalism?" I believe his observation was not only correct but that the implications of this reality have been tremendously significant in this country and, to the point of this discussion, higher education. Evidence of this condition is so ubiquitous that I will not take time to build a case here. In short, consumer capitalism reasons that we are what we own, our hopes and dreams, and the solutions to the world's most pressing problems are material, and individuals and markets must be manipulated for the purpose of increasing consumption. Though these assumptions are troubling on several levels, they are particularly troubling when connected to higher education.

Higher education—once aspiring to be the province of the search for the good, the true, and the beautiful—has now largely succumbed to the ideals of the marketplace. Regretfully, the values and priorities of the marketplace are not congruent with the traditional values and priorities of the academy. While this point could be addressed in a variety of ways, perhaps most relevant to the focus of this monograph, consumer capitalism treats students as customers, and it is impossible to care, at least in the biblical sense of care, for customers. Customers are valued because they have something we want (money), and they will give it to us in return for a particular product or service (a diploma). A Christian educator cares for students because they have inherent value and because God has entrusted a portion of their care to us. We honor God by doing our best for our students whether or not they appreciate it or see the value in what we ask of them. Consumer capitalism assumes the customer is always right, but a caring community recognizes that sometimes students must be asked to do or consider things they do not wish to—for their own good and for the higher goods that our institutions exist to accomplish. While seeing a student as a customer leads us to try to keep them enrolled at any cost, a caring community seeks to help students discern God's calling—even if that leads them away from our institution. Caring for students is much more complex and driven by much different ends than caring for customers. Acknowledging these differences and guarding against the strong temptation to give in to this way of thinking is essential in maintaining the integrity of communities of care.

Conclusion

These are unprecedentedly difficult days on college campuses, and this reality may be truer of small residential Christian colleges than others. The challenges are financial, philosophical, competitive, social, and more. However, perhaps the greatest challenge is a crisis of purpose—there is little agreement inside or outside of higher education for why it even exists. Whether or not they are acknowledged or even recognized, organizations and movements always have a goal or a purpose or—in the words of Postman—an end. He suggested that a worthy end "is a transcendent, spiritual idea that gives purpose and clarity to learning" (Postman, 1996, p. 5). I would add that such an end also gives purpose and clarity to educators and educational leaders in their practice of caring for students. The current inability of higher education as a whole, and of many institutions individually, to articulate a clear reason for being is a serious hindrance to providing meaningful education. Education that lacks a reason for being cannot care well for students. Communities of care must have a meaningful purpose that is consistent with the means used to accomplish it.

Though these theological foundations of care are crucial, caring communities also have many practical necessities if they are to exist. One of the most essential elements is knowing our students well enough that we have the opportunity to listen to them and to speak into their lives. Caring for students means we will listen to them as they tell us what they value, what they hope for, what they fear, and what they need. We must be present enough in their lives to attend to them as they wrestle with and process these things. As we listen, they may ask us to speak into their lives. We must recognize and take seriously the fact that, as educators, we have a prophetic role in the lives of our students. We have to remember that their desires (like ours) have been misshapen and misaligned as a result of living in a fallen world—and so caring for our students will not always mean legitimizing their "felt needs." Sometimes, challenging students in what we perceive to be wrong thinking, wrong valuing, or wrong acting is the truest indication that we have heard and genuinely care for them.

The sort of caring that we envision is more than fixing students' problems or even helping them develop the tools to fix their own problems. The kind of care envisioned and commended by this monograph aims to direct students toward optimal, holistic health and well-being—what we sometimes call flourishing. And though such care will indeed yield great personal benefit for our students, ultimately our purpose is not just to help them for their own sakes, but also to equip them to function in a manner that empowers them to contribute to the well-being of those around them and the world at large.

Nicholas Wolterstorff gave us a magnificent answer to the question: What is the purpose of higher education? He reminded us that we are *Educating for Shalom* (Wolterstorff, Joldersma, & Stronks, 2004). In other words, we are educating our students to bring about justice, righteousness, peace, and heavenly order. Tim Keller (2010), writing about shalom, said,

> God created the world to be a fabric, for everything to be woven together and interdependent. Neil Plantinga, a theologian, puts it like this: "The webbing together of God, humans, and all creation in equity, fulfillment, and delight"—[this] is what the Hebrew prophets call shalom. We translate it "peace," but in the Bible, shalom means universal flourishing, wholeness, and delight. It describes a rich state of affairs in which natural

needs are satisfied and natural gifts are faithfully and fruitfully employed, all under the arc of God's love. (para. 9)

In a world in which so much communication is mediated by technology, where life is lived at hyperspeed, where the meanings of words such as "relationship" and "friendship" have been compromised by our immersion in social media, in which there are limited natural connections between the young and old, and where "new" and "novel" are more valued than "timeless" and "abiding," fragmentation is the order of the day. Though as inhabitants of this culture we find this disintegration dismaying, as educators we must find in it a teachable moment. As the poem "Winter Solstice" (n.d.) suggests:

Even as brilliance must have a stage
So darkness gives radiance its age
It is lightlessness and storm that renders hearth its charm.

The challenging climate we inhabit offers Christians and Christian higher education the opportunity to cultivate communities of wholeness and coherence that will provide nurture for our students and exemplary models of care to our partners in the academy: for the good of both, we would do well to give ourselves to this task.

References

Astin, A. W. (1977). *Four critical years.* San Francisco, CA: Jossey-Bass.

Australian Government Department of Health. (2004). Young people and drugs—issues for workers. In *Training frontline workers: Young people, alcohol & other drugs* (Module 11.6.1). Retrieved from http://www.health.gov .au/internet/main/publishing.nsf/Content/7C6EE8947A8BD4C5CA257 BF00020455D/$File/m11lw.pdf

Fish, S. (2004, May 21). Why we built the ivory tower. *New York Times.* Retrieved from http://www.nytimes.com/2004/05/21/opinion/why-we-built -the-ivory-tower.html

Garber, S. (2007). *The fabric of faithfulness: Weaving together belief and behavior.* Downers Grove, IL: IVP Books.

Hamrick, F. A., Evans, N. J., & Schuh, J. H. (2002). *Foundations of student affairs practice: How philosophy, theory, and research strengthen educational outcomes.* San Francisco, CA: Jossey-Bass.

Keller, T. (2010, October 26). The beauty of biblical justice. *ByFaith: The Online Magazine of the Presbyterian Church in America.* Retrieved from http:// byfaithonline.com/the-beauty-of-biblical-justice/

Mistler, B. J., Reetz, D. R., Krylowicz, B., & Barr, V. (2012). *The association for university and college counseling center directors annual survey.* Retrieved from http://files.cmcglobal.com/Monograph_2012_AUCCCD_Public.pdf

Parks, S. D. (1986). *The critical years: The young adult search for a faith to live by.* San Francisco, CA: Harper & Row.

Parks, S. D. (2011). *Big questions, worthy dreams: Mentoring emerging adults in their search for meaning, purpose, and faith.* San Francisco, CA: Jossey-Bass.

Postman, N. (1996). *The end of education: Redefining the value of school.* New York, NY: Vintage.

Sumiano, B. (2018, January 19). Can colleges engineer relationships? *The Chronicle of Higher Education,* A14.

Willimon, W. H. (1997). Religious faith and the development of character on campus. *Educational Record, 78*(3–4), 73–79.

Winston, G. C. (1997). Why can't a college be more like a firm? *Change, 29,* 5, 32–38.

Wolterstorff, N., Joldersma, C. W., & Stronks, G. G. (2004). *Educating for shalom: Essays on Christian higher education.* Grand Rapids, MI: Eerdmans.

Zimmerman, J. (2017, November 3). High anxiety: How can we save students from themselves? *The Chronicle of Higher Education,* A52.

EDITORS

Timothy W. Herrmann is Professor and Graduate Director of the Master of Arts in Higher Education and Student Development program at Taylor University (Upland, Indiana). Tim has also served in a variety of other roles, including Dean of Assessment, Associate Professor of Psychology, and Associate Dean of Students. In addition to being a former President of the Association for Christians in Student Development, he is also cofounder and coeditor of *Growth: The Journal of the Association for Christians in Student Development*. Tim's publications include *A Parent's Guide to the Christian College: Supporting Your Child's Mind and Spirit during the College Years* (2011), *Funding the Future* (2012), and *A Faith for the Generations: How Collegiate Experience Impacts Faith* (2015).

Emilie K. Hoffman is the On-Site Director of the Irish Studies Programme for Taylor University, based in Greystones, Ireland. She received a bachelor of science in nursing and addictions counseling from Indiana Wesleyan University and a master of arts in higher education and student development from Taylor University. Emilie has worked in mental health nursing, university residence life, living learning programs with inner-city youth, and leadership of a student support team at the University of Canterbury Students' Association. Her research interests include student learning dispositions, living learning communities, cross-cultural experiential learning, and theological exploration of vocation.

Jessica L. Martin completed her master of arts in higher education and student development at Taylor University (Upland, Indiana) in May 2018. She graduated from Palm Beach Atlantic University (West Palm Beach, Florida) in 2016 with a bachelor of science in medicinal and biological chemistry and a minor in biblical and theological studies. Jessica's research interests include the marketization of higher education, student consumerism's impacts on learning, and developing learning dispositions.

Hannah M. Pick serves as Executive Administrative Assistant to the Vice President for University Relations at the University of Portland. She is also a freelance editor and writing consultant for academics throughout the greater Portland, Oregon, area and at Taylor University in Indiana, from which she holds a master's degree in higher education and student development. Hannah's research efforts have touched diverse areas of higher education, including learning dispositions, writer identity, and academic departmental culture. Among other publications, Hannah served as an editor for the previous volume of the ACSD monograph series and recently published a review in *Christian Higher Education* of Andrea L. Turpin's *A New Moral Vision: Gender, Religion, and the Changing Purposes of American Higher Education* (2016).

Kirsten D. Riedel serves as a residence director at Belmont University in Nashville, Tennessee. Her research interests and work in higher education are focused on understanding connections among institutional culture, purposes, and priorities as well as challenging students to explore questions of meaning, purpose, and calling. She holds a BA from Whitworth University and an MA in higher education and student development from Taylor University. Kirsten was also an editor for the first volume of this monograph series, *A Faith for the Generations: How Collegiate Experience Impacts Faith* (2015).

Kelly A. Yordy is the Program Services Director for the Master of Arts in Higher Education and Student Development program at Taylor University and previously served in residence life. Kelly earned her PhD in higher education leadership and administration at Indiana State University. Her research interests include faculty stress and work-life integration, women in leadership, ethic of care in higher education, and historical research on deans of women.

CONTRIBUTORS

John Foubert serves as the Dean of the College of Education at Union University. He previously served on the faculties of Oklahoma State University and the College of William and Mary, in addition to administrative posts at the University of Virginia, University of Maryland, and University of Richmond. Dr. Foubert also serves as the Highly Qualified Expert and Senior Advisor for the U.S. Army Sexual Harassment and Assault Response and Prevention program at the Pentagon in Washington, DC. His most recent book is *How Pornography Harms: What Teens, Young Adults, Parents, and Pastors Need to Know* (2016). He appears regularly in the media and speaks often at Christian colleges on the topics of sexual violence and pornography.

Anita Fitzgerald Henck has served as Dean of the School of Education at Azusa Pacific University since 2011, after five years in APU faculty and chair roles. Previous areas of her service have included Vice President for Student Development and Retention at Eastern Nazarene College in Quincy, Massachusetts, and Assistant to the Provost at American University in Washington, DC. Her areas of research and consulting include leading change in higher education, organizational culture, leadership transitions, and building effective teams.

Tabatha L. Jones Jolivet is an Assistant Professor in the Department of Higher Education at Azusa Pacific University, where she teaches doctoral-level higher education courses on critical issues, diversity and social justice, and the nature of research inquiry. Her research focuses on campus activism, faith and spirituality, inclusive and socially-just organizational change, and the prevention and reduction of sex and gender-based violence. A higher education leader, community organizer, teacher, minister, and speaker for twenty years, she previously held positions as Associate Vice President for Student Life, Title IX Coordinator, and Associate Dean of Student Affairs. She is working on a collaborative book project that explores the intersection of race, religion, and higher education.

Karen A. Longman is the PhD Program Director and Professor of Doctoral Higher Education at Azusa Pacific University. She also serves as a senior fellow of the Council for Christian Colleges & Universities (CCCU), where she worked for nineteen years as vice president for professional development and research. In 2016, Longman's contributions to Christian higher education were recognized through her receiving the John R. Dellenback Global Leadership Award. Longman coedits *Christian Higher Education: An International Journal of Research, Theory, and Practice* and an eight-volume book series being sponsored by the International Leadership Association focused on women and leadership; she also coedited the first volume, titled *Women and Leadership in Higher Education* (2014). Most recently, she worked with a group of more than twenty chapter authors to publish *Diversity Matters: Race, Ethnicity, and the Future of Christian Higher Education* (2017). She holds a PhD in higher education from the University of Michigan.

Larry Markle is the Director of Disability Services at Ball State University, where he oversees the university's efforts to provide access for over a thousand students with disabilities. During Larry's tenure as director, Ball State has been recognized as a "disability-friendly" institution—one of a select group of schools going above and beyond legal mandates. Larry is involved in several professional organizations, including the Association on Higher

Education and Disability (AHEAD), and is a past president of Indiana AHEAD. He serves on the review board for the *Journal of Postsecondary Education and Disability* and was also the project director for "Ensuring a Quality Education for Indiana's Students with Disabilities," a grant funded by the U.S. Department of Education, Office of Postsecondary Education.

Donald D. Opitz is the campus pastor and a Professor at Messiah College. He is an ordained minister in the PCUSA with a PhD in religion and culture from Boston University. Don's work in ministry has been focused on college students, and his work in the classroom has ranged widely (theology, leadership studies, social theory, higher education) while exploring the connections between faith and learning and life. Along with Derek Melleby, Don wrote *Learning for the Love of God: A Student Guide to Academic Faithfulness* (Brazos, 2014).

Sharon Daloz Parks is Principal of Leadership for the New Commons and a Senior Fellow at the Whidbey Institute in Clinton, Washington. She holds a BA from Whitworth University, MA from Princeton Theological Seminary, and doctorate from Harvard University, the Divinity School. Her publications include *Big Questions, Worthy Dreams: Mentoring Emerging Adults in Their Search for Meaning, Purpose, and Faith* (Tenth Anniversary Edition, Jossey-Bass/Wiley, 2011); *Leadership Can Be Taught: A Bold Approach for a Complex World* (2005); and she coauthored *Common Fire: Leading Lives of Commitment in a Complex World* (1997). She currently teaches in the Executive Leadership Program in the Albers School of Business and Economics at Seattle University, and she speaks and consults nationally.

Miroslav Volf is the Henry B. Wright Professor of Theology at Yale Divinity School and the Founder and Director of the Yale Center for Faith and Culture. He was educated in his native Croatia, the United States, and Germany, earning doctoral and postdoctoral degrees (with highest honors) from the University of Tübingen, Germany. He has written or edited more than twenty books and over ninety scholarly articles. His most significant books include *Exclusion and Embrace* (1996), winner of the Grawemeyer

Award in Religion, and one of *Christianity Today*'s 100 most important religious books of the twentieth century; *After Our Likeness* (1998), in which he explores the Trinitarian nature of ecclesial community; *Allah: A Christian Response* (2011), on whether Muslims and Christians have a common God; and *A Public Faith: How Followers of Christ Should Serve the Common Good* (2011). His most recent books, *Flourishing: Why We Need Religion in a Globalized World* and *Public Faith in Action: How to Think Carefully, Engage Wisely, and Vote with Integrity* (coauthored with Ryan McAnnally-Linz), were published in 2016.

Roger D. Wessel is a Professor of Higher Education in the Department of Educational Studies at Ball State University in Muncie, Indiana. He also serves as the Director of the Master of Arts program in Student Affairs Administration in Higher Education and on the doctoral faculty for the Doctor of Education program in Adult, Higher, and Community Education. Prior to serving in these roles he worked in enrollment, career, orientation, and evaluation positions with higher education. His graduate degrees are from Southern Illinois University at Carbondale, with undergraduate degrees from Lee University and Tomlinson College. His research agenda includes research on persistence to graduation for students with disabilities, and he serves as the Executive Editor for the *Journal of Postsecondary Education and Disability*.